DADDY

Reflections of Father-Daughter Relationships

An Anthology of Personal Essays and Narratives

Edited by Dr. K E Garland

DEDICATION

For women in dysfunctional father-daughter relationships, you are not alone.

For fathers of daughters, you matter.

ACKNOWLEDGEMENTS

A concept is just a thought, without people to bring it to fruition. So, my only thank you is to the fourteen women who were brave enough to write their stories and trust every step of this process.

TABLE of CONTENTS

PART I

Hurt people hurt people ~ Yehuda Berg

A LETTER TO MY FATHER
Varina Price

Remember this: Whoever sows sparingly will also reap sparingly, and whoever sows generously will also reap generously. 2 Corinthians 9:6 (New International Version)

After years of trying to figure out who he was, I was ready to put it all on paper. I was ready to write words that described my feelings with little empathy toward his. After all, I'd spent over thirty years separating truth from emotions. I'd made several attempts to gather my pain and throw it over a cliff. But I couldn't. A constant void occupied my life. He was there, even though I couldn't see him. I was often reminded of his presence. I heard about him. I heard all about the family trips. Shooting guns, fishing, camping, reunions, and family functions were plentiful. But I wasn't there, nor was I invited. Instead, I sat in the corner and hid tears behind my sleeves. I spent so much time trying to understand why he never invited me. Why couldn't he just pick up the phone and call or text? One day, after all the hurt, I wrote him a letter in hopes that my pain would just go away.

***

Dear Daddy,

I always wondered what it was like to be a "daddy's girl." What would it be like to run to you and sit on your lap as you helped me tie my shoe, tell me a story, or give me a hug? Oftentimes, I'd ask friends and family. What is it like to have your father around for school events, family vacations, or evening dinners?

Over the years, I've tried to reminisce about happy times we've shared, only to realize we have none. It's crazy. The memories I have of you being present are limited. But I do remember times you wouldn't come home from work. Mom would pile us in the car, and we would look for you. She made it a game. On several occasions, we found you standing around a bonfire, beer in hand, laughing with your friend, Donny, and a few women. Mom couldn't hide her distress. I also remember the time Mom and I came home with groceries, and she sent me inside to ask you to help. I walked in on you and uncle doing lines of coke on Mom's glass perfume tray.

I've tried to recall birthday parties where you didn't have a drink in hand. I've tried to remember celebrations where you stood around the table singing "Happy Birthday." The times are few. I spent my adolescent years trying to be your daughter, forcing my time with you, only to be treated like a ghost.

You will never realize the magnitude of pain that has scarred my life. Decades have passed, and it's apparent we will never be able to create the bond I've yearned for. I am thirty years old, and I don't even know you. What makes you happy? What are your favorite hobbies? What is your passion for life? What's even more depressing to me is you have no idea who I am nor have you made a consistent attempt to find out.

Do you love me? I've wondered this my entire life. After much thought, I've decided the answer is no. I suspect the only reason you and I talk a few times a year is because I am your daughter. Perhaps you feel the sense of obligation, but sometimes I think you hope your phone calls go to voicemail so we can both forgo the awkward silence. Unfortunately, the lack of any sort of relationship between us has confirmed my worst fears. The only tie you and I have is your name on my birth certificate.

Maybe I'm wrong. Perhaps I have an illusion of what a father-daughter relationship is supposed to be. But I see the love you and your son share. I see the relationship between you and your other daughters. Why haven't you and I ever shared something similar? Why was I the only outcast? I'll never have fond memories to reminisce upon or share with family and friends. You have missed out on so much of my life and who I am, yet you seem to have no curiosity to ask.

Now that I'm a parent, I can't imagine how my children would feel if I was not a significant part of their lives. I could never abandon them as you have me. We've shared an endless amount of memories, and I know we will make more. It's important to me that they remember I was constantly involved and that I cared. But you don't feel the same about me.

Remember your response when I told you I was going back to school to become a nurse? I do. First you asked, "Why are you going back to school?" Then you said, "You went to school to do hair and don't even do that. Now you want to be a nurse? You're probably not going to do that either."

I believe as parents we have a responsibility to praise our children and remind them to fulfill all their dreams regardless how far the reach seems to be. But you obviously don't think so. You doubted me. You spoke against my goals, and even though I've made it, you have yet to acknowledge my achievements. Despite your discouragement, I invited you to graduation. You said you would try to get that day off from work, and I was hopeful. However, a week before commencement, you couldn't take the time off because you had to save money for medical bills. Let me fill you in on what you missed. I was a double major. I have two degrees, and I attained three of the highest honor societies. I was recognized for it all at that graduation.

9

Disappointment is the only expectation I have from you.

You and I will never have that elusory father-daughter relationship. Your inconsistent attempts prove it. I've accepted it. You've tried, but I question your efforts. Do you remember randomly calling me to create an email account or to change your password? Or how about that time you asked me if phone numbers could be traced so you wouldn't get caught? Or do you remember all the times you asked me which of my friend's moms were single? Do you remember asking me to drop you off at that house late at night and then instructing me not to tell anyone about it because it was a friend's ex-girlfriend? Sadly, this list can go on.

I have sought counseling over the years to try and fill the void where our relationship should be. I wanted to learn to trust people who come into my life. Unfortunately, I still struggle with it. I have terrible commitment and trust issues, especially with men. I am so afraid they are going to up and leave. Before that can happen, I push them away. When something is going good I fear it will be temporary and quick to disappear. I read somewhere that a father-daughter relationship can have a profound impact on what a woman seeks when she is ready for a committed relationship. I've compared our relationship with the times men have approached me with commitments, and the cycles mirror each other. I've treated men how you've treated me. Initially, I showed interest, and when they got too close, I vanished. The more they pushed for something, the further away I ran. That's us. That's our cycle.

But not anymore. These past few years, I've stopped trying, and look where that got me. We speak once or twice a year.

The therapist advised that I speak to you about it. I've tried and never found the right words. Will this letter help? I don't know. I can't lose something I don't have. In fact, I don't even expect a response. But if you do read it, I'd like you to take a few moments and really think about what I've said. If you feel anything, then take those emotions and imagine what I've experienced every day for over twenty-five years.

No matter the outcome of this letter, I wish you nothing but happiness.

***

He never responded to the letter. Over a year passed before I heard anything from him. Usually he called the day after my birthday or the week following. But that year, my phone rang on the actual day. His name flashed on the screen. Not Dad, Daddy, or Father, but his name. I sent the first call to voicemail. The second time I answered, and he acted as if we were the best of friends.

He sang me his typical "Happy Birthday" song, "and many more on channel 4 and *Looney Tunes* on channel 2. Happy Birthday! I just wanted to call and tell you. Okay. Well, I just got to the yard. I'll call you tomorrow or something."

That was it.

It wasn't the phone call that changed my state of mind. It was the silence that led me to believe there was nothing. We had nothing to talk about. He had nothing to ask after a year of silence. I cried a little bit after that phone call. Those tears were the result of a lifted weight. I cried because my fears were true, and I was finally okay with that.

Today, I see him just as I think he sees me, an acquaintance. All I needed was confirmation of our relationship and time to digest it. He is not my father. He is not someone I look up to or someone I hold dear to my heart. He was a stranger during adolescence, and now during adulthood, by choice. He has become a social friend at gatherings. We share a few words, an awkward side hug or pat, and that's it. Reality has set in, and I no longer cry about the fact that I do not have a father figure. Rather, I smile knowing that I am done mourning. He no longer paralyzes that part of my life.

A DAUGHTER'S GRACE
Tikeetha Thomas

After traveling to Tennessee the previous week, a visit to the therapist was necessary. Exhaustion overwhelmed me, but I needed to see her. I was emotional. I needed an explanation for these odd feelings. I suffered from anxiety. She invited me to sit down and describe what happened.

***

Tennessee

American dining options were limited in our small town, so we drove to a nearby city to eat. We walked into the local Applebee's. We sat in the same section we did last year.

Dad wasted no time. He looked at me and said, "So Daughter, do you have anything to ask me?"

I paused and sipped my water before responding, "No. Do you have something you want to tell me?"

He shook his head. "No, but you have my undivided attention. I wanted to talk to you."

"I'm listening."

"My dad, your grandpa, had twenty-two children," he started. "My mother had eight. Of those eight, your uncle, Charlie, and I are the only ones who have the same mother and father. When I was growing up, I wanted to be just like my dad. I never saw him much because he moved to Chicago when I was young. He would just swing by when he was in town and give my mom some sex."

The story absorbed my attention.

He stopped for a moment and then continued, "He was the man to me. I wanted to be just like him when I grew up."

The waitress came by our table and asked for our orders.

"Order for me, Daughter. I don't know what to get."

I sighed. "Dad, I don't know what you like. What kind of food do you normally eat?"

"Anything is fine."

I ordered double-glazed baby back ribs with fries for him. For me, the classic burger and fries. He continued the conversation.

"I didn't think there was something wrong with wanting to be like my dad. My dad always seemed so cool."

He smiled, lost in reminiscing. I cleared my throat.

"I didn't have role models," he continued. "My parents were my role models. I didn't know they weren't the ones I should follow."

"Daddy, I hear what you're saying about not having good role models to follow, but when you become an adult you have to accept responsibility for your choices. You can't blame your parents for your shortcomings. You fathered nine children with six different women. You married other women and never divorced my mom. You weren't responsible. You weren't a father to many of your children. We were the forgotten ones. What made you think that was a good choice?"

"I know, Daughter, but I didn't know better."

I shrugged my shoulders and responded, "We all have choices, Daddy. I chose not to be the kind of parent to my son that you were to me. I chose to put my education first so any children I had wouldn't suffer if my marriage didn't survive. Choices, Daddy. We all have them."

He looked at me and nodded his head in agreement. "I've made some pretty bad choices, Daughter."

"You have, Dad," I blurted out.

His expression shifted from smiling to somber.

"I look at my life and realize that you're the only one of my children to have anything to do with me. You come and see me faithfully. Twice a year. No one else comes to visit," he admitted.

My frustration rose. I couldn't take it. I couldn't feel sorry for him. He left me. He left my siblings. He abandoned us. He chose not to be a part of our lives. His regrets over his poor choices in life were not my problem. His excuses for his parents' promiscuity and his decision to repeat the pattern were part of his broken family story, but he could have chosen differently. Where was his accountability?

I sipped my iced tea.

I needed to change the subject. "How's your health, Daddy?"

Another topic might stop the anger, hate, and disappointment that bubbled in my stomach. "Are you taking your medications?"

I had forgiven him. I did what God had told me to do. What more could I do?

"You following the doctor's orders? How are you?"

He smiled and replied, "Yes, Baby. I am. I sit back in my room at your grandmother's house and think all day about my life. I wonder how my life could've been different. How I could have been different if I made different choices. I think about how I missed your high school graduation. I wonder how you were when you graduated that day. I think about that day. I think about the emotions and experiences that I had when I graduated from high school, and I wonder what was going through your mind when you graduated from high school. Were you happy? Were you like me and just ready to get the heck out of school?"

The words tumbled out. "I graduated from college, Daddy. I got married. I had a baby. I got divorced. There were many more life-changing experiences that I had besides my high school graduation."

He nodded. "I know, but that's what I think about." He sipped his soda. "I remember watching you when you were younger and smiling because you were my oldest girl. I knew that you would be something special."

Pain seeped into every cell of my body. Tears flooded my eyes and stopped just short of my lower eyelids.

I looked at him and said, "You know what I remember? I remember getting dressed in my Sunday's finest and waiting for you to show up to visit with me and my siblings. You were in Maryland that weekend for a wedding, and you promised that you would come see us. We were so happy. We sat there waiting for you for hours, and you never showed. You never called to say that you couldn't make it. You forgot us. Again. The pain of being forgotten was so unbearable to me. You didn't care."

The years of pain couldn't stop me from continuing on my rant. "I remember not having enough food to eat because my siblings wanted seconds, and my mom made ten dollars too much to qualify for food stamps. I remember the disappointment of an empty fridge and empty cabinets, at not having enough food. If you had only paid child support or gave any support, our lives could have been different."

The words flowed like a relentless storm. "Do you know that one of my many psychological issues stems from me not having enough growing up? I hoard food. I always need to see a stacked refrigerator or cabinets. I waste food. It scares me to think that my son would ever go hungry. I have fifteen credit cards. Not that I need them all, but the fear of being too poor and not being able to afford something scares the hell out of me. I am a mess, Daddy. I'm broken. Just like you."

He stared at me. And then he cried. Publicly. I'd never seen him look so sad. His pain was irrelevant. Years of wounds and emotional scars covered my heart. I thought I'd healed, but I couldn't stop describing hurt after hurt. Each word cut like a knife through all my scar tissue. I had a new mission. My assignment was to share my aching heart and make him see the effects of his actions. He'd broken me.

I wanted revenge.

He had to see that I didn't need him.

I wiped my eyes before continuing. "Daddy, you chased so much ass all your life, and look at you now. No one is here with you. Not one woman you abandoned your children for is here to take care of you when you're sick. You put women above my siblings and me, and now you have nothing. I'm more successful than you and probably some of the women you chased, and I'm sitting here buying *you* lunch. I don't date men who can't afford to pay for meals, yet here I sit, spending money on you. You haven't spent a dime on me in almost thirty years, but I am being a dutiful daughter and trying to be here for *you*. To spend time with *you*. To get to know *you*. Heck, I'm feeding *you*. But, you know what? If I wasn't saved, I would tell you to kill yourself. You have wasted your life."

The pain in his eyes said I'd gone too far.

"Thank God I'm saved."

But I didn't feel saved. A saved person wouldn't have said that. I'd acted like a brat. I was hurting, and I wanted him to hurt too.

***

Maryland

My therapist looked at me as I held back tears.

"You haven't forgiven your dad," she said.

Was she crazy? Wasn't she listening to how painful my visit back home was? Didn't she hear me say I'd spent time and money on a man who wanted nothing to do with me while I grew up? I had forgiven him. I was doing as God instructed.

I dismissed her comment. "Yes. I have forgiven him."

"No," she said. "What you've given him is grace. If you had forgiven him, then all the things he said and remembered would not have bothered you. You would have responded, 'That's okay, Dad.' However, you are still so consumed with pain, and it's understandable, but you haven't forgiven him."

Her words sunk in.

For the last four years of my life, I believed I'd forgiven this man like God wanted me to do. God gave me a word on what I needed to do. I failed. I failed God. I hadn't realized it until now. My stomach felt queasy.

"I never knew that people could give grace. I thought only God gave grace, but I see what you're saying," I said to my therapist.

"What does forgiveness look like to you? What do you need to do to forgive him?" she asked.

"I need to not have a relationship with him. I need to release him from my life and pray for him. I need him gone."

"And that's okay too," she reassured. "You have to protect your heart and spirit."

That day, I left her office more confused than ever. My life was not what I thought it was. I'd advocated for others to live their truths, but I didn't know my own. I thought I was incapable of giving grace. Grace was something so superior and angelic that I thought only God could provide it.

But I was wrong.

I've realized I need to do as God instructed and forgive my dad. Forgive him for the years of abandonment. Forgive him for being who he is. Forgive him for not being who I wanted and needed him to be. Forgive.

Forgiveness isn't the same as grace. The only way that I can get to the point of forgiveness is to extract him from my life. To extract him from my son's life. To pray for him. To truly wish him the best. To heal.

THE THING ABOUT MY FATHER
Anna Scott

The therapist sat across from me, hands folded on her lap, listening as I complained about my father again. She appeared thoughtful. Or maybe she was bored.

"He barely pays attention to me, and when he does, it's all so superficial. I'm sick of it, sick of pretending that we have some kind of relationship when the truth is, we don't. He hardly knows me."

She paused and asked, "What is your father's ethnic background?"

I hesitated before answering, wondering what the hell this had to do with anything. "Italian."

Her facial expression changed from thoughtful to all-knowing. "Ah, that explains it. Italians generally value their sons more than their daughters. This doesn't have anything to do with you personally. It's cultural."

I eyed her with suspicion. Could this be true, or was she feeding me a line of bullshit so I'd stop whining and get over it? Probably it was the latter, though I had to admit, when my parents divorced, my father insisted my brother live with him after he remarried, whereas for me, this was optional.

Still, I wasn't entirely convinced of her theory until I watched *The Sopranos* one evening. The popular show chronicled the life of Italian mob boss, Tony Soprano. During the episode, Tony's teenaged son complains to his older sister that their parents care more about her than they do about him. His sister corrects him.

"We're Italian, A.J. You're their son. You'll always be more important."

I went still when I heard those words. Could the therapist have been right after all?

I still held on to a twinge of disbelief, until my father recounted a popular story from his adolescent years. When he turned sixteen and got his driver's license, his parents bought him a fire-engine red, convertible sports car with white leather interior. During summers, he would drive it to the shoreline where his grandparents owned a cottage. He and his cousin, whose parents had bought him a speedboat, would spend the summer waterskiing and cruising around. One day, my father parked the convertible at a boat launch and forgot to put on the emergency brake. His vehicle rolled into the ocean before he could stop it.

I'd grown up hearing this story and had seen photographs of the car, but it wasn't until my grandmother died that my father told me the rest. He had braced himself for the terrifying task of telling his parents, certain he'd be reamed out and punished for life.

"Honey, don't worry about it. The car can be replaced. The important thing is that you're all right," his mother said.

Hearing this sealed the deal for me. My father, the only son in an Italian family, was a beloved prince who could do no wrong. My aunt, his sister, was loved, but not spoiled. The therapist must have been right. It had to be an Italian thing.

***

After my father divorced his second wife, my brother, Tim, now an adult who suffered from mental illness, moved in with him after years of living alone in apartments and then a group home. People called my father a saint for this arrangement, but I knew better. The generous disability checks my brother had been receiving since his honorable discharge from the military paid half the household bills.

The arrangement lasted until my father retired and moved to Florida. Tim went with him, and it was decided he should have his own place again. Living with a mentally ill person wasn't easy, and Dad had a girlfriend now. He set my brother up in an apartment close to the condo he'd bought and kept a close eye on him.

Eventually, Dad remarried for a third time, and he and his wife started coming up North for a couple of months each summer. They stayed at her condo, which was about thirty minutes from my house. Tim rented a studio apartment located in a gritty section of a nearby city.

This is when the real trouble between my father and me started.

When he arrived each year, usually in late June, I would invite him and his wife over for dinner. They would stay for about two or three hours, leave, and I wouldn't see him again until he was preparing to head back to Florida in August, gracing us with another two-hour visit.

The first few summers, I reasoned that we didn't see each other more because my job was so busy that time of year. Also, my father spent most weekdays and Saturdays selling boats at his cousin's marina. However, he found time to golf regularly and to take day trips with his wife. Several times I reminded him that although I was busy, his grandsons were around with plenty of time on their hands. He was more than welcome to pick them up and spend an afternoon with them. He never did.

Once, hoping to get him to pay attention to at least one of his grandsons, I called my father in Florida and asked if I could send my teenager to visit during his February vacation. Silence met my request.

"Have you mentioned this to him yet?" he eventually asked.

"No, I wanted to run it by you first."

A long pause, then he completely changed the subject as if I'd never asked. I was too stunned to bring it up again.

That following summer, he paid us the usual two obligatory visits and made no additional effort to see his grandsons. I didn't understand. His own parents had been the most attentive, loving people in my life. I'd spent countless weekends at their house being doted upon and loved unconditionally. Had my father not learned anything from their example? I wanted to call him out, but whenever I attempted to say the words aloud, it was as if some invisible force physically prevented me from being able to speak.

Then one night I got a phone call that changed everything.

My former stepmother, Marian, was clearly drunk. This in and of itself was shocking because in the years that she'd been married to my father, I'd never seen her take a drink. In fact, on several occasions, she made it known that one of the main reasons for the disintegration of their marriage was my father's excessive drinking.

"Lissen ta this," she said, her words slurred. Then she told me something no daughter should ever know about her father.

He had cheated on her with his secretary, the woman who was currently his wife. The two of them had engaged in threesomes with people they found through ads on the Internet. Marian found this out when she went through his emails one night. In one of them, he told the third woman that she would be able to spot him because he'd be wearing a bright green sweater.

"And lissen ta this," she said, lowering her voice to a near whisper, though I'm sure no one was around to overhear her. "That night before he goes out, he's wearing the green sweater and says ta me 'How does this color look on me?'"

I wanted to throw up. I stayed on the line a while longer only because I couldn't speak. When I finally found my voice, it was to make an excuse to hang up. I never told anyone what she told me, not even my husband. I wanted to forget that I'd ever heard it.

***

The following summer, my father visited us without his wife. It was hard to look him in the eye after what I'd learned.

"Marian must be drinking again," he said. "She gained back all the weight she lost. She looks horrible. She's bloated, and her face is all red."

"What do you mean drinking *again*?" I'd assumed her drunken phone call to me was an isolated incident.

"She's a drunk. You didn't know that?"

Realization, along with sadness, washed over me. This explained her descent into obesity, all the times she'd canceled our plans because she didn't feel well, and the chronic misery she wore on her face. I decided not to mention her phone call.

"How would I know this? I've hardly ever seen her drink."

He explained that about halfway through their marriage, Marian started closet drinking heavily. She would wait until everyone was in bed, take out the bottle of vodka she kept hidden in the cupboard over the stove, and drink until she passed out, often on the living room floor. Sometimes she became violent when he tried to bring her up to bed. The only time she would have sex with him was when she was plastered.

"Why didn't you get her help?" I asked, though I already knew the answer. If he got her help, he would have to face his own drinking problem and personal shortcomings. Better to let her stay passed out on the living room floor than be forced to alter his lifestyle.

He shrugged and took a sip of the drink I'd made him. "She didn't want help."

After the initial shock of his disclosure wore off, I became suspicious of his motive for telling me this after years of silence. Maybe he'd heard that Marian was phoning people while drunk and exposing his dirty little secrets, so he was trying to discredit her. I wanted no part of his manipulative mind games.

In late September, back in Florida after another summer of ignoring us, my father phoned. While I listened to him babble on about himself, as usual, I knew the time to call him out had arrived. I had finally found my voice. It was fueled by anger and disgust. I managed to keep my voice calm.

"Dad, how come you hardly see me or the boys when you're here in the summer? We only see you twice, maybe three times all summer. You never pick up the boys alone, even though I've told you they're around. It's like you don't want to spend time with us."

I waited, breathless, for his response.

"I didn't realize you felt that way."

I took a deep breath. "Well, I do. Honestly, I hate having such a shallow relationship with my father, and you're really missing out on what great grandkids you have."

We spoke for another minute and then hung up. I turned to my husband. "Did I sound okay? I didn't sound mean or accusatory, did I?"

My husband, who was also fed up with my father and insulted that he didn't want to spend more time with our sons, said, "You sounded fine."

With that settled, I breathed easier. I'd done it. I had spoken my truth. Whatever the outcome, there was that.

The next day when I checked my email there was a message from my father.

"I couldn't speak freely because [my wife] was in the room. Now let me tell you what I really think…"

He launched into the most mean-spirited tirade I had ever been the recipient of. He accused me of never reaching out to him unless I needed somewhere to stay when I was in Florida, and of not minding my own house well enough, a reference to my teenaged son's marijuana use. He called me horrible names and said I was always at war with someone, all while making himself out to be the world's greatest father.

His words landed in the pit of my stomach like dead weight. When I could move again, I forwarded the email to Marian.

"Oh boy," was her reply.

I also read it to my husband.

"I hate to say this," he said, "but your father is an asshole."

That was it, of course. My husband was right, and to his credit, it had taken him over twenty years to say so. My father was an asshole. He always had been. An asshole disguised as a charming Italian prince.

I chose my words carefully when I replied. There was no way I was going to stoop to his level.

"All I did was speak my truth and tell you how I've felt for years. You're the one who had to insult me and call me horrible names. Don't worry, I won't ask to stay with you the next time I'm in Florida. I don't need you."

I resolved to stop speaking to him. I didn't care that he'd been forced into a shotgun wedding at eighteen years old because he'd gotten my mother pregnant. I didn't care that when I was a baby, he used to rock me in his arms and sing Frank Sinatra songs to me. I didn't care that he'd taught me how to play chess and strum "Smoke on the Water" on the guitar.

All I knew was that when he left us when I was eight years old, I became nothing but an obligation to him. He picked me up every other weekend, but mostly I spent the time with my grandparents, and later, my stepmother. He never called during the interim to ask how I was. His child support checks bounced more often than not. He was mostly a stranger to me, more like an uncle that I saw occasionally.

The weekend after Thanksgiving, Marian came over to visit. It was unseasonably warm, so we sat outside sipping beers. Apparently, she was done pretending that she didn't drink.

After a while, she said, "You know, you not speaking to your dad is eating him up. He's not getting any younger. Maybe it's time to forgive him."

I was stunned. How could she defend him after the way he'd treated her? There was so much I wanted to say in that moment, none of it kind, but I refrained.

Instead, with all the coldness I felt, I said, "I don't feel sorry for him at all. He brought this on himself with his nasty email and the neglect of his family."

After a long moment, she said, "All right then. I won't bring it up again."

She didn't. In fact, we have hardly spoken since that day.

At Christmas, I finally caved in and called my father. I didn't like living with bitterness. He sounded so happy to hear from the kids and me. We acted like that ugly email exchange had never happened.

The following summer, he made more of an effort. He took my teenaged son kayaking. He brought my youngest son to the driving range a couple of times. The summer after that, it was business as usual.

I hosted a Father's Day picnic. We had lunch out one day, and that was it. I accepted it for what it was, knowing that at least I'd tried.

Little did I know that my father had yet to hit an all-time low.

***

My mother was visiting Tim in Florida when she called me, upset.

"You won't fucking believe this."

My stomach sank. "What?"

"Tim has been giving your father five-hundred dollars a month since they moved to Florida."

I went still for a moment, trying to process what she'd said. They'd been in Florida nearly ten years. "What are you talking about?"

"I was talking to Tim, and he mentioned that he gives your father five-hundred dollars a month. I asked him why, and he said because dad asks for it so he gives it to him."

A myriad of emotions streamed through me: anger, disbelief, sadness, outrage. At the same time, I wasn't surprised. "Are you going to confront him?"

"Of course."

My father's excuse was that it was hard taking care of a mentally ill adult child, and he couldn't work because of it. When they first moved to Florida, he'd been broke living on his pension only, and the money was in exchange for taking care of Tim. My mother reminded him that he was still taking the money, despite getting social security, being remarried, and his wife having inherited half a million dollars when her father passed. He blew up. He called her a shitty mother who had neglected Tim his whole life, then hung up the phone.

I was furious when she told me this.

"That is bullshit. If Tim takes up so much of his time, why did he work at the golf course part-time for years after they moved to Florida?

Why does he work six days a week at the marina in the summer, which is his excuse for never seeing us? He is totally full of shit. I wonder if his wife knows about this." I suspected not, given the nasty email he'd sent me.

This was far worse than threesomes behind Marian's back. This was taking advantage of a mentally ill child who trusted him. There would be no turning back for my father now, no redemption. The man was going to hell.

***

The next summer, I never once saw my father alone. He kept his wife close like a blanket of protection. It was his way of making sure I couldn't confront him about what I'd learned. He needn't have bothered. As sickened as I was by my mother's revelation, I chose to stay out of it. This was between my father, brother, and mother. Ultimately, the man had to live with himself and face his maker one day.

My mom's disclosure to me, however, helped me finally come to terms with my relationship with my father. My therapist had been right that I shouldn't take his neglect personally, though I'm convinced it has less to do with him being Italian and far more to do with him being an asshole. The man doesn't get it, and he never will. He completely lacks self-awareness. He doesn't value his family; even my half-brothers hardly see him. He is a hedonist whose own pleasure and comfort comes before the needs of others.

I can now understand and accept these things without internalizing it. I have learned that my self-worth and value are not contingent upon my father's love, or anyone's love, and that some relationships can only be sustained when we stop having expectations.

ABANDONED AT BREAKFAST

BB

First Trimester

My heart dropped when the blue letters flickered across the screen. It plainly stated "pregnant"—no lines or pluses or minuses. I had Googled symptoms of being pregnant at least half a dozen times before buying a test to confirm my inhibitions. However, I still wasn't convinced after sitting on the toilet for ten minutes, staring at the word spelled out before me. So, I ripped open another test and proceeded to pee on a second stick. My anxiety escalated as each small circle illuminated from left to right, until finally, "pregnant" was digitally displayed on the screen, again.

I walked downstairs to my boyfriend, Shawn, who was awaiting the results, and said in a pleasant yet understated tone, "I'm pregnant." I cracked a smile and waited for his reaction. He kissed me, rubbed my stomach, and remarked, "I can't wait to meet S3!"

Two lost souls in three apartments over four years, it was inevitable that a baby would add more imbalance to our lives. Living together had brought about the instant gratification of casual sex, shared responsibilities, and a sense of security. However, the newness of sharing a home had worn off, and I found myself in the trenches of an identity crisis. I was struggling to see who I was outside of my relationship. I wanted Shawn to love me even if I mistreated him, and I repeatedly sabotaged his efforts just to see if he would stick around.

When I felt he did not meet my needs, the tempered little girl came out like a needy child crying out for attention from her mother and father.

I expected him to be my lover, my friend, my voice of reason, and my support system—even though I did not do those things for him. By the end of the first trimester, we hit rock bottom.

I moved out.

Second Trimester

After a few days, I broke down and told my friends that Shawn and I had split. But, I kept the details about our unborn child a secret and close to my heart.

Then, I called *him*. Daddy. I called to let him know that I had moved in with Mom for the time being.

"Are you okay, Babe?" he responded in a concerned voice.

I lied and told him I was fine. I reassured him that I would remain in touch with him. We talked at least once a month about work, the latest news, or any pleasant memories from the good ol' days—rarely anything heavy. We would get each other laughing hysterically about his addiction to Pepsi or that one time he flipped the lady a bird when she cut him off during our road trip to Virginia.

But a week later, having had enough of the secrecy, I decided I had to tell him I was pregnant. I wasn't sure how he'd respond, especially since I already told him about Shawn and me but failed to include this detail.

"Dad, I'm pregnant."

He quickly responded, "Oh, really? What are you having?"

I told him we just found out we were having a girl. He was elated with the idea of having a granddaughter. News of my pregnancy sparked a series of weekly check-ins from him, but I was burdened with the thought that he did not offer to come see me. He played it safe by sending weekly texts and making the occasional phone call to check on me. He was present on some level and absent on most others. On my worst days, I felt an unexplainable sense of abandonment, which sent me into a frenzy of emotional turmoil. I wondered if maybe I only loved men who would never completely love or accept me.

I must've been in the shower for over twenty minutes, tears streaming down my face, mixing with the water traveling down the drain. I tried washing them away by running my face through the water, but I could still taste the salt from my tears. Bitterness and hurt remained. My body and its baby bulge shook in unison as I wept and panted hysterically, wrinkled fingers wiping my face. The green tile covering the shower walls blurred. My lens on life was hopeless. In that moment, it was clear to me that the life I had in mind did not exist.

I had always pictured living a traditional life—definitely a husband and two kids—a dog and white-picket fence would be a bonus. This was a familiar memory of a time when I was happy. My family was whole when we had this profile, even without the fence and the dog. We were complete when it was my mom, dad, brother, and me. We lived in Jacksonville, Florida, for eleven years. No dog, no fence; just the four of us occupying space together where we managed to love, grow, and live. Life felt normal when Mom signed school forms and managed doctor appointments while Dad reviewed homework and taught us how to defend ourselves.

On Friday nights, we would raid Blockbuster's aisles looking for newly-released videos. Then, we would stay up all night watching movies and wake up to Daddy's famous pancakes on Saturday mornings. The laughter and togetherness of those Blockbuster nights are some of my fondest memories. But those memories are tainted by thoughts of sadness from overhearing loud arguments between Mommy and Daddy about our finances. I distinctly remember seeing the look of resentment on her face after he lost his job for the second time. The insults, name-calling, and door slams got worse as it became more obvious their marriage was coming to an end.

We struggled financially, yet the spiritual strife in our house was just as daunting. Jehovah's Witness *Watchtower* pamphlets were scattered on the coffee table while church bulletins lay nearby. Every Sunday morning felt like warfare in our house, and my brother and I were stuck in the middle. After Mom expressed her disapproval of me and my brother going to Kingdom Hall, we attended a nondenominational church with her instead. Mom had visited the Kingdom Hall once, but she felt it was best if we went to church with her. So, Dad went to the Kingdom Hall every Sunday, alone.

Sometimes when he and I were alone, he would ask, "What are you going to do when Jehovah comes back during Armageddon?" I usually responded by telling him, with a lost look on my face, that I didn't know. The four of us were already stuck somewhere between hell and Armageddon. But, in spite of it all, it seemed I was happiest when we were stuck together.

That night in the shower, pregnant and bawling, I was undoubtedly nostalgic. Those four walls of the shower served as the only place I didn't have to pretend I was crying tears of joy about my daughter's arrival. Some days, resentment and regret crept into my heart because I knew she would be a living reflection of my past transgressions. She would soon arrive to bear the burden of shame and guilt with me. But thankfully, she was cocooned for now, at least until I could get my feelings sorted out.

I was broken. While I intended to address my feelings, all I could do was suppress the hurt that filled my head and heart. My thoughts kept coming back to how *he* wasn't around to father me during my pregnancy. Worst of all was the realization that I, too, had failed. I hadn't been able to break the cycle of the single-parent home. I imagined my daughter growing up in the same environment I had. She would come to know that a half-empty closet meant the void of the belongings of one of her favorite people. She would not experience the joy of residing in a home where Mommy and Daddy shared space together. She wouldn't know the comfort of much-needed family time with her immediate family members each morning and evening.

As I reflected back on life after my parents' divorce, I was still clearly emotionally conflicted. Before my brother and I had the chance to deal with the dissolution of my parents' marriage, we were given the ultimatum of staying in Jacksonville with Daddy or moving to Atlanta with Mommy. I can't replay in the exact details of that conversation in my mind because I've subconsciously blocked it from memory. All I can recall is the sound of my mom's voice asking if we were staying or leaving.

We left.

But now, very much pregnant and crying in the shower, all of the stuffed emotions seemed to be surfacing all at once. I was being forced to deal with it. Every tear was for Daddy. I inhaled and exhaled as a way to make sure I was still alive and as a way to breathe life into the baby girl I was carrying. This meltdown made me realize how much I missed his presence and how much I was torn by his absence.

From that point forward, I made it a habit to journal my feelings when I felt myself reliving those moments that spilled out in the shower. I normally kept a calm demeanor, so a sporadic breakdown in front of friends, family, or even strangers was met with surprise—although I could easily blame it on my raging hormones. I also held back because I didn't want to verbally expose the imperfections that had gotten me to that point. I was clearly an emotionally wounded person.

Third Trimester

I was seven months pregnant, and the date of my baby shower was approaching. I casually told Daddy the date without directly asking if he would attend. I had written down the name of every anticipated attendee on a yellow piece of notebook paper, but a question mark was placed next to his name.

During one of our weekly calls, he confirmed my suspicion when he simply said, "Babe, I won't make it this time." And as usual, I let him know that I understood. But in the back of my mind, I was trying to grasp how he thought it was acceptable to not make it *this time*, as it would be the only time I would be celebrating the birth of my first child.

Most times, I felt numb to the disappointment when Daddy couldn't attend events, particularly when we moved to Atlanta. After all, he was more than three hundred miles away from us. So, over the years, I built an impenetrable wall that would keep me guarded from any unforeseen headaches and heartaches. But the lurking wounds only grew deeper, and I unknowingly began to tally up the number of letdowns I had sustained throughout the years. A deep-seated resentment was taking hold.

The baby shower took place in December in a clubhouse filled with pink balloons and other girly knickknacks. Friends and family bought more than enough gifts for our sweet baby girl. I was very thankful to be surrounded by the cutest handcrafted blankets, but most importantly, by our "village" who would help raise our child. Even with all the gifts at my feet and with everyone at my beck and call, I still felt that familiar sense of emptiness.

Behind the makeup and flashing cameras, I was still the little girl who longed for her father's embrace. I wanted him to accept me and tell me that I was beautiful, even fifty pounds heavier. I wanted him to grab my cheeks and say he hoped my baby girl's cheeks would be as fat as mine. But he didn't. So, I just tried to remain grateful for the gift he sent.

Birth

She was born from the safety of her internal haven into the depths of a winter morning on her exact due date, January 13, 2014. Two unfamiliar faces welcomed Nylah. Soon she would come to know us as her mother and father.

Our sweet baby girl greeted us at six pounds, six ounces. Tears fell without my permission when they placed her on my chest. She was so small and delicate. I wasn't ready. My feelings weren't sorted out. She was no longer cocooned from the brokenness that plagued me. Nylah was exposed to my imperfect world, and now it was her world too.

We announced the news to friends and loved ones through a combination of calls and text messages. Between nurse checkups, I finally got the chance to return Daddy's phone call. He said that Nylah had been born on the same day as his mother. I would not have known since Daddy and his family are Jehovah's Witnesses and therefore didn't celebrate birthdays. I hoped their shared birthday would create a kindred bond and make it a day he could never have an excuse to miss.

Our weekly calls continued, but they felt empty when he said he wanted to see Nylah but would not follow through with concrete plans. Over Nylah's first year, I shared her milestones with him through a series of text messages. He missed out on being there to change a diaper. He couldn't see weariness in my eyes when nights and days blended. He missed it all.

By her first birthday, Nylah was developing an emotional bond with her grandparents. I was grateful for that support system, but I wanted her to know her other grandpa. Even though I had hurt festering in my heart, I still wanted to make room for him to be in her life. I didn't want him to lurk in the background of his granddaughter's life, but unfortunately, it seemed that was the direction the relationship was headed.

He didn't come to her first birthday party. I realized that January 13 wasn't as significant as I had thought it would be to him. I came to terms with the idea that I couldn't force him to form a relationship with his first grandchild. But, I had taken all I could bear. Daddy had struck out—and I didn't have the emotional capacity to handle another letdown.

I was too afraid to call him as I secretly feared he would leave forever after hearing what I had to say. But I simply had to confront him. It wasn't as diplomatic as my imaginary conversations with him. I pictured us sitting face-to-face so Daddy could see the expression of his heartbroken little girl. I wanted him to be within arm's reach, so I could feel his warm embrace of apology after I let him know how his absence affected how I viewed myself and my relationships leading up to that point.

But, I didn't know the next time I would see him, so I ended up texting him a long message. I told him how I felt about him not being there when I needed him and how his lack of involvement in Nylah's life affected me. After I hit send, I sat there expecting Daddy to call or text me immediately, but I didn't hear from him for three days. I spent those three days constantly peeping at the phone, waiting for any indication that Daddy cared. I thought letting him know how I felt may have been a mistake. I thought maybe Daddy felt what I had to say wasn't important enough. I was consumed with feelings of abandonment and rejection.

Finally, the phone rang. I was nervous. I honestly did not want to pick up the phone because I didn't know what Daddy was going to say to me after three long days. Why had he waited so long to call me? I wanted to sound confident when I finally picked up, but all I could manage was a mumbled, hesitant hello. Daddy was calm when he greeted me with the usual "Hey, Babe." He revealed that he was so hurt by what I had said that he had to take time to respond to my message. Daddy expressed that he wanted to be there for me and admitted that he was focused on his own desires. He said that he genuinely didn't mean to hurt me and that the divorce with Mom wasn't my fault. He talked a little about his absence when my brother and I were younger and owned up to several of his mistakes. Lastly, he assured me that he wanted to develop a relationship with Nylah.

Once Daddy expressed his feelings, I reiterated some of the points from my text message. I also told him that it hurt my feelings that he did not come to Nylah's first birthday party. Daddy sounded empathetic and promised he would be present for both me and Nylah going forward. I knew Daddy wasn't perfect and that it would take some time to restore our relationship. Our conversation served as the first step toward reconciliation.

In short order, he made plans to come see us. Still a little skeptical, I made sure to mentally prepare myself for a last-minute disappointment. I held my breath up to the minute he knocked on the door. But after that first knock, I was at ease. His presence filled the space as soon as he walked through the door. I smiled when he embraced Nylah because I saw the younger version of myself that yearned for his affection.

We still don't see Daddy as often as I would like to, but Nylah knows who he is now. She hasn't yet shared in the pleasure of waking up to his pancakes on Saturday morning, but at least I know that when she does she won't be sitting at the table with a stranger.

Two years after rebuilding a relationship with my father, I'm not perfect, but I no longer love from a place of bitterness and brokenness but rather from grace and forgiveness. Healing wasn't instantaneous, but the process of it was a necessary piece of me being a better mother to Nylah. On top of that, I was able to reconcile with Shawn, and we got married. My relationship with him was far from perfect, but I realized I had to stop blaming him for the hurt that Daddy caused me. Shawn was there—for Nylah and me.

SUNDAY PUNCH
Kotrish Wright

"Hey! Where the fuck do you think you're going?" Dad asked.

"Just for some fresh air," I replied.

My mom and dad had been arguing since the sun set. It was a typical Sunday with Dad. He was drunk and yelled about her letting another man rule his kingdom. In his mind, she listened to the pastor more than him. He was upset. I'd learned to ignore his ritual. Thank God I was just a few months shy of my eighteenth birthday. Soon, I'd be waving goodbye to these infamous Sunday arguments.

I could hear them from where I sat in my grandfather's old bedroom. We lived together in my grandparents' house. I stood up, left the room, and headed out of the house. Dad was on my heels, so I didn't shut the door. I sat on the porch, waiting for him to catch up and unload on me, knowing it was useless trying to sneak out.

"Get your sorry ass up, and shut the front door!" my dad instructed. "Walking around like you don't have any home training," he continued. "Close the fucking door."

"Sorry," I said as I quickly pulled the handle. "I didn't want to shut it in your face."

I sat back down.

"Who the fuck are you talking to?" he asked.

BAM! His right fist connected with my face.

"Don't hit my child!" Mom screamed as she flung open the door.

It was too late. He had punched me in the face. He'd swung before I could blink.

That was it. I'd had enough of his shit, and I was getting the hell out. I leapt up, head throbbing, and dashed back in the house to call my sister.

"You need to come get me," I said plainly.

Meanwhile, my dad stepped on my heels, pushed me, and knocked the bags out of my hands, insisting I wasn't going anywhere.

"Call the cops!" Mom yelled from the room across the hall. This was also a part of the ritual. I called, but I sensed this time would be different. This time he hadn't just mentally, emotionally, or verbally abused me. He'd put his hands on me. According to the case management staff and law enforcement I'd spoken to on other occasions, nothing could be done unless things became physical.

The officer showed up moments before my sister did. Dad started his typical Sunday speech.

"She's an unruly teenager trying to run my house."

I'd heard this rant and what followed on many previous Sundays. "She needs discipline," he'd always say.

Then, there was the finale. He'd look at me and offer a suggestion, "Talk to her, Officer, maybe even alone."

But this time, the script changed.

The officer looked at my dad and said, "That's not a bad idea. I'll talk to your daughter and wife, then you. Why don't you step out on the porch for me?"

Wrong move.

My dad flipped. Yelling at the officer, he said, "You don't have the right to ask me to step out on the porch! I'm staying right here and listening."

The officer asked three times. My dad refused.

"Mama!" he shouted.

My grandmother came out of her room. Her son's commotion and abuse over the past few hours elicited no emotion, but seeing a white police officer in her living room was enough to make her wail aloud, "Oh, Lawd!" She immediately broke into tears.

The officer requested a fourth time, and still Dad wouldn't budge.

"You are refusing authority," the officer told him, and he slammed Dad against the ground.

My heart broke. Wait, that's my dad. Don't hurt him.

He's drunk and has some mental health concerns, I thought. But that's no reason for all this. Dad and the officer wrestled on the ground. For a moment, I feared he would be shot that day. He wasn't, but the handcuffs were cranked on him extra tight. He cried from the pain and pleaded for them to be loosened.

The officer pointed to me and said, "Maybe this one gets her unruliness from you 'cause you clearly have a problem with authority."

Huh? I'm not unruly. I'm the victim. In that moment, a seed of sadness planted itself within me. It was as if I was to blame. Everything was my fault.

What followed only served to deepen my pain and confusion. The officer required each of our versions of what happened. Mom spoke slowly as she described the day's events. But, it was when she got to the part where I'd walked outside that I was dealt another blow.

"I saw him swing. But I don't know if he actually punched her or not."

"What?" I said. "You were there! You even yelled, 'don't hit my child.'"

The stinging blow surfaced. I'd been hit twice that night. Betrayal. Hurt. Mistrust. Pain. Loneliness. Vulnerability. Each took its place in my heart. After the cop talked with me, he took my dad to jail. Everything was my fault.

My grandmother kicked me out that night.

"You're not welcome back in my home," she added.

Like a homeless kid, I sat outside with my bags surrounding me and waited for my sister and mom to finish discussing logistics. I needed somewhere to sleep.

That night my sister drove me to my maternal aunt's house where I slept on the couch. Two days later, she woke me up at four in the morning. The Department of Children and Families wanted to talk with me. She refused to have them in her house. I had to go.

On top of that, my grandmother informed all of my cousins, aunts, and uncles on her side of the family that I'd sent my dad to jail. Soon after, each one wanted me to retell the story. Each interrogation ended with the same advice: lying will catch up to you! Everything was my fault.

While I couch-surfed at other maternal family members' homes for the next few weeks, Dad was released from jail. Mom had ensured I missed the court dates because I told her I wouldn't follow her coaching this time. I wouldn't lie about what happened that Sunday.

"Kotrish, I can't pay these bills by myself," she said, as if that was some kind of excuse for not defending me.

Once again, my sense of betrayal resurfaced. I knew that my mom brought in the majority of the funds, and furthermore, who cares? I was her daughter! I was hurting. I had to attend school and act like nothing happened. Mom and the social worker spoke on my behalf, and since I was almost eighteen and would soon be able to make the decision to talk to him or not, the judge simply issued a no contact order.

I was alone. A no contact order with Dad ultimately meant no contact with Mom. Thanksgiving that year, I called my mom, hoping to see her. She and my dad spent the day celebrating together. Then she spent the remainder of the day with Dad at his job. As for Christmas, everyone ate together as a family, except me. I spent the holiday riding around with friends avoiding trouble.

***

About six months later, after the no contact order had expired, I was in the car with both of my parents, driving down the highway. We were headed to Daytona where I had a final speaking engagement for the Career Education Clubs of Florida. I watched my dad puff up his chest for no apparent reason, and then moments later, out of the blue, arrogantly admit punching me in the face that Sunday. Mom's silence filled the rest of the space. I looked out the window. Trees and billboards blurred.

My hate for men intensified all the more that day. My dad was supposed to be my protector, my template for a future husband, but instead he engraved his name as perpetrator in my heart, mind, and memories. For the next nearly decade of my life, I begged and pleaded for him to build a healthy relationship with me. That never happened, and I'm not sure it ever will. For me, time has run out.

TRIAL BY FATHER

S.R. Toliver

In medieval times, trial by ordeal was a normality. Although a barbaric way to judge guilt or innocence in modern society, it used to be a common practice because those in search of truth believed that divine powers would intervene and ensure the triumph of the righteous. A person's culpability was determined by subjecting them to oftentimes life-threatening experiences. If the accused was blameless, the person would prove his or her virtue by escaping injury or death. I remember discussing the various trials—by combat, by cold or hot water, by ingestion, by fire—during a unit on the Salem witch trials in my high school English class. It was silly to me to think that judgment could be arbitrarily passed based upon frivolous exercises of domination and power. Yet, as I've gotten older, I realize just how much my life path was determined by a trial, one that challenged the trajectory of my being.

Before I started high school, I used to visit my father every summer for at least a few weeks, and at some point in the vacation we would always end up at my aunt's house in Texas. She had a country ranch-style home, large enough for a family of five, with a garage that looked like it hadn't actually contained a car in years due to the amount of clutter stuffed into every crevice. It was the ideal location for a visit because even though she had enough space for many people, her household was a family of one. I believe she had a yard, but you'd never find me in it. July summers in Texas were much too hot for my northern blood. The daily average was well over ninety degrees in that part of the South, and my hometown in Pennsylvania barely reached the mid-eighties most summer days.

To combat the heat, I often wore shorts and some form of summer shirt—halter top, T-shirt, midriff, tank top—the normal attire for a fourteen-year-old girl on a hot summer day in Texas. I will never forget the way my melanin-infused skin burned from the heat, the way it consistently darkened as the days passed, or the way it peeled if I stayed outside for more than a half hour.

My father often treated me and my siblings like we were tourists visiting his homeland, and his attempts at introducing us to his Texan culture often required us to leave the comfort of air conditioning. He would take us to the zoo, to amusement parks, to the movies, and sometimes to the mall. Of course, these are excellent options, but in retrospect, I believe these outings were either his way of pretending that the dullness of adult life didn't exist or his attempt at tricking us into enjoying our time with him.

One summer day, he told us that we were headed to the mall to get my sister, brother, and me out of the house. I remember him mentioning this trip early in the morning, so I got dressed right away rather than lying around in my pajamas, which was and still is one of my favorite things to do. The chosen style of dress for the day was a red-and-black striped midriff shirt with a pair of black shorts and some tennis shoes. As an additional adornment, I had my signature bang plastered to the left side of my face with mounds of gel to hold it in place. I also had a low ponytail—if one could call it that since the hair that fell from the hairband was about two inches long and barely touched my neck.

For some reason I don't recall, we finally left for the mall around three. I had been waiting around all day, dressed and ready to go. I don't think I was impatient by any means, but the idea of waking up with the promise of an early activity only to have to sit and wait around for the activity to commence can make anyone antsy. By the time we finally got in the car to leave the house, I had lost all motivation to go. But, of course, as this was a family outing, I joined the ranks and took my seat in the car.

The mall's interior design was standard in structure. Storefronts lined the walkways; colorful and enticing visual displays acted as physical advertisements. Mall patrons briskly navigated their way past each other in search of some unspecified item.

Initially, the four of us traversed the halls together, but my sister was twelve and my brother was nine, making for some very different shopping preferences. Because I considered myself close to adulthood at this point—what fourteen-year-old girl doesn't—I asked if my sister and I could branch off from the boy unit and go shopping by ourselves. My mother allowed us to if we consistently kept in touch by phone, so I assumed that we would have the freedom to do so here as well. I was correct.

We perused the stores in search of that one shirt, dress, or pair of jeans that made us stop in our tracks and commit to a purchase. After about an hour, we began to realize that our search would be fruitless; there was nothing that piqued our interest, and it seemed like this was going to be a wasted mall excursion. We decided to stop wandering and make a plan instead. We didn't want to go back to following the guys around, and we weren't hungry, so we made the decision to do nothing—a common resolution for adolescents in the mall, which is probably why rules against dawdling are so prevalent.

While my sister and I were loitering, a pair of young men came over to strike up a conversation. I was at a socially awkward stage in my life, so I wasn't sure what to do in this situation. Of course, I had spoken to boys before, but this was different. Should I flirt? If I do, how do I flirt? What should I say? I really hadn't been in many situations like this, so I didn't know what to do with my hands, my feet, or my facial expressions. I hadn't been taught the proper way to interact with boys. In all honesty, I was excited; a boy wanted to talk to me, and he wasn't asking me to join his sports team or talk to him about the latest episode of *Dragon Ball Z*.

This confusion lasted only a moment, for as soon as I had gotten the courage to finally speak, an obscure pain shot through my upper arm. When a volunteer goes to give blood, the nurse wraps a rubber band tightly around the donor's arm to restrict the blood flow, causing the veins to swell. In the same way, my arm felt an intense pressure, but instead of awaiting a needle, I experienced only the piercing stab of a fingernail. I was completely taken by surprise because I had no idea who would have grabbed my arm so tightly. Who would be putting such pressure on my arm, causing it to throb? When I turned around I discovered that it was my father's grip that was causing so much pain.

Numerous thoughts crossed my mind, the first of which was an intense recollection of every single thing I had done in the last twenty-four hours that could possibly have led to such a reaction. I went through every action, every movement, every utterance, and I could think of nothing. I thought back over the course of the last week, and I could think of nothing. I thought back to the beginnings of the summer, and I could think of nothing. OK, I didn't make my bed a few times, and I'm pretty sure I talked back a time or two, but nothing I had done could have caused such a tight hold, such a sharp pain, and such emotional turmoil.

Before I could ask and have my questions answered, my father spoke, and I received my reply.

"Go buy yourself some new clothes. You're out here looking like a whore," he said as he threw money at me.

I wish I could say that the paper bills fell to the floor and never touched my face, but that would be a lie. They hit me physically and cut me mentally. I wish the bills would have caused some form of physical pain to accompany the psychological agony I felt.

A father had chosen to publicly call out his daughter on her appearance, and his reasoning for this was because I was dressed like a harlot, a loose woman. But why he had immediately chosen this recourse confused me. Why—after being in this clothing all day—had my outfit just now offended him? What did I do within that moment that prompted his discontent? What about my existence in that space made him treat his daughter like a stranger? What had I done to make him think that I had no respect for my personhood? So many questions.

His expression was stale, no emotion. The answers I needed weren't going to be found in those hard eyes. And although I can't say this is the first time I've seen that look on his face, I was still surprised. I needed a reason, an explanation to help me understand why he responded in that way. I should have known my longing would prove fruitless, as it always had, for his actions often didn't require explanation. Once I received a spanking because my cousin hurt himself playing outside. I asked why I was going to be spanked as I walked to the dresser to pick out the belt that would cause me pain. The answer was mainly because I hadn't stopped my cousin from hurting himself. These were the answers I was used to, and in this current situation at the mall, I shouldn't have expected anything different.

The worst part of this experience was making the decision about what to do next. Confronting him for his egregious allegations could cause further discontent for me, and although picking up the money and buying something else to wear would appease my father, I felt like I would be admitting to wrongdoing. It was a catch-22. Either way, I would be emotionally scarred and mentally impacted by the decision I would be forced to make.

Was I guilty of harlotry by my choice of clothing in a public space? Should I tell him how wrong he is and risk greater repercussions? I wrestled with these questions for what seemed like an eternity, and although I wish I would have had the courage and confidence that I have now to speak to him about his misconceptions and educate him about the woman his daughter was, I didn't. I picked up the money. I went to the nearest store. I bought a baggy shirt and some jeans as tears streamed down my face. I felt I had failed the trial.

The rest of that day was a blur. I don't remember what happened after I paid for the new clothes. I mentally shut down. Never in my life had I felt like I was nothing. I was so accustomed to the love my grandfather and mother gave me, instilling in me a sense of self and purpose. But on this day, the girl who existed before that summer went into hiding the moment the money changed hands at the store counter. The vibrant, inquisitive, and slightly nerdy girl shriveled up. The fire within her faded, and her trust in authority figures diminished.

The next few years were filled with misinformed notions. I didn't trust myself to be a "good girl" anymore. I came to believe that I had made a choice that summer day to dress that way because I wanted the attention. I forced myself to think that it wasn't that hot and that I could have chosen something else to wear. I took my father's comments to heart and truly let those words guide my actions. I changed. I created an artificial self based on my father's comments.

Of course, during this time, my mother, grandfather, aunties, and siblings were there for me as I struggled, but I never let them truly see what was happening inside or why I felt like tarnished goods. It was hard for me to articulate these feelings. How was I to explain that my father publicly humiliated me by calling me a whore and throwing money in my face? If I said it aloud it made the comment real all over again; it gave the words vitality when all I wanted was for them to dissolve into nothingness. I veiled my inner agony in an attempt to promote the death of my emotional pain. I thought that if I didn't speak about it, then it would go away. I didn't address it. I let the psychological wound fester.

But finally when I was eighteen, I let out all my pain, anger, and frustration. My father had called because he disapproved of a piercing I had gotten, once again spewing hatred about how I was acting like a whore and promoting myself to men in ways that solicited unwanted attention. It was at this point, after his long tirade against my indecency that I finally let four years of pent up anger flow from my mouth. Although I don't recommend anyone create the combinations of words I used to tell him how I felt, I will say that letting him know how much I hurt and why I hurt was the most freeing feeling I've ever had.

When my lecture was finished, I hung up the phone. I was emotionally drained, and I was physically tired, but I was done, literally and metaphorically. After that phone conversation, I restricted conversations with my father to special occasions. As time went by, the stifling of communication dwindled further from special occasions to only a couple calls per year. Today, he is completely blocked from contact. For my self-care and the promotion of my self-worth, I had to end communication with him. But, I can't lie and say that it wasn't a difficult decision, for there is no easy way to dismiss a father from one's life. However, in order for me to navigate this world without the burdens placed on me by a man who was supposed to uplift instead of depress, I had to let go of my father.

In medieval ordeals, the trial by water proved guilt or innocence based on one's ability to survive submersion. If the defendant floated to the top, he or she was guilty and hanged. If the accused sunk to the bottom, he or she was declared innocent while hoping to be rescued from the bottom. In my own trial by father, my culpability was determined by being subjected to a painful and unpleasant experience. I was thrown into submersion of guilt and shame, and although I nearly drowned in self-deprecation for years, I was ultimately dragged out before I was too deep. I was given a trial, and I came out of my ordeal scathed but free.

THE DEPRIVATION OF A FATHER'S LOVE
Ishna Hagan

I'd always known my father to be a great financial provider despite never having lived with him. Whenever Mama insisted that I call and ask him for money for school clothes, he sent a $300 check. When I needed a new pair of prescription glasses, which cost upwards of $350, he sent the money. For me, visiting him meant financial plenitude. I was never broke. As a ten-year-old, I oftentimes had more money than some of the adults in the small town where he lived. In fact, he was commonly known for being financially well-off; consequently, this ended up being the basis of our relationship.

It wasn't until after childhood that I realized something was missing. My father and I didn't share an emotional connection. The reality of this sunk in more deeply as I entered my teenage years, and it bothered me.

When I visited him, we had very little conversation. We didn't play games. We didn't read books together. He never dressed me for anything. He never gave me advice. We didn't do so little as hug. Those types of interactions were just not our thing. But at thirteen, I knew it was odd. I desired physical affection from my father. I wanted to spend time with him, laugh with him, share ideas with him, trust him, and see his love. Otherwise, how would I know if he did?

Right around the time I'd began longing for an emotional bond with my dad was about the same time he began to stop giving me as much money. Sadly for me, it was at a time I needed to be supported the most. I was headed to college.

***

In August of 2006, I'd finally generated real excitement about going to the university. My eagerness bubbled up as I arranged my side of the dorm room. Enthusiasm always kicks in right in the moment of my experiencing it— like, this is real! That day in Argo Hall at the University of West Florida was surreal. I was officially a college freshman! The realization was exhilarating, and I had to share it with my loved ones. My father was one of the first to come to mind.

"Hey Dad, I'm in Pensacola. The trip was five hours, pretty smooth. My roommate and I are setting up our sides of the room. Anyway, I'm calling to let you know about all this stuff I just learned I have to pay for. Meal plans, books, binders, transportation. Tuition is ridiculous. I'll be working part-time in the library but was wondering if you can send funds to help out?"

I thought he'd be understanding and proud of my achievement, and consequently, willing to help me through college. I'd already envisioned his response: Of course I can help, baby girl. It's your first year in college, and you've worked hard to get there. I'm sure you know that I can't pay for your full tuition, but I can help you purchase some of your books or pay for your meal plan. I'll also send you a care package of some college essentials.

I was sorely mistaken.

My dream conversation was farfetched. He told me he would not be able to help at all. He had retired and didn't have the money. The foundation of our relationship had crumbled in an instant. Eighteen years old meant that the one form of support he'd given, and that I'd grown used to, was completely over. My dad had financially cut me off, and it was all at once the new standard for our relationship.

I took it hard when he declined to help. All the effort that goes into making it to college and the amount of money it requires to earn a degree—my father had decided that it didn't matter to him and was not his problem. It tossed me into a flurry of emotions. I wrote a letter to him saying that I'd make it without him no matter what. I meant it, but as time went on, I knew I'd handled the situation in a rude and inappropriate way because I'd been hurt.

Instead, I wish I would have written a letter explaining that what I really wanted was his affection, guidance, and involvement. I wanted him to embrace me when I was at his home. I wanted him to protect me from wayward teenage boys. It would have been great to have some pointers about dating men or for him to show up to one of my many sporting events.

When I went to college, I wanted him to express how proud he was of me and to be there to support me. The issue over money for tuition was just an additional dagger in my heart. When it comes right down to it, all I wanted was to be sure of the fact that he loved me, and I wanted to hear him say it. I never heard it once.

***

As time went on, due to the dysfunction I experienced, I built a wall around my emotions with everyone, not just my father. The deprivation of his affection caused me to learn how to keep people out. I became adept at moving on from being disappointed by him and eventually all men. In part, I started to feel like I didn't need a man, period. Romantically, if a relationship didn't work out, it did not matter to me. I'd be fine. Goodbye. Moving on.

However, I knew when I said I was fine, I was lying. I had started a bad pattern of maintaining an emotional distance from men. As an adult, I decided this was not the way to go, and if I kept this behavior up I would never be able to have a healthy relationship with a man, including my father.

After all I'd been through, I realized that underneath all the layers of painful emotions was a hurting child. I'd been wounded by my father's lack of affection, and it made me detached. I realized that in order to heal, I needed to start being honest with him, and all men, to repair, build, and strengthen my relationships. I knew if I continued to improperly process and express my emotions, it wasn't going to fix anything. I finally started taking steps in a more positive direction. Nowadays, I am well-rounded in my way of thinking. I'm grateful that I faced my problems head on and chose to do something about them. My issues with my father no longer govern me.

PART II

If you want others to be happy, practice compassion. If you want to be happy, practice compassion ~ Dalai Lama

MARSHMALLOW
Charise Kollar

After Christmas Eve dinner, my grandfather used to rustle through the woods behind my father's house while wearing a Santa Claus costume, shouting "Ho, ho, ho." The jingle of the bells on his belt buckle would roll down the mountain terrain, gracefully tinkling in our ear drums, a sweet reminder of magic's existence. For years I did not notice Pa excusing himself early from dinner and returning just in time for dessert. I was preoccupied with the prospects of presents, sugar, and Claymation Christmas specials.

When the last bite was taken and the last fork fell, my father was always right on cue. "Did you guys hear that?" he'd whisper to everyone at the table. "I think I heard the bells."

My eyes would widen. Santa was here.

As I bolted to the edge of the property line, marked by trees tethered together along the cliff's edge, my father would slowly walk after me, shuffling his feet behind my quickened pace. When he caught up to me, he would lift me up and wrap me tightly in his arms, my head reaching above his. I'd sink into his embrace, comforting me like a warm blanket. My father was like a giant marshmallow—round, sweet, and gentle.

The winds sweeping off the hills were always fierce and frigid in winter. The cold was almost unbearable. But I was looking for Santa, gosh darn it. Nothing would distract me. It was my job to listen for the bells, and I took that job seriously.

"I can hear you, Santa!" I'd shout.

"We can hear you, Santa!" my father would echo. "Merry Christmas, Santa!"

Like a distant whisper, I could hear him moving through the trees.

"Ho, ho, ho," I could hear him say against the blowing winds and the ruffling of the trees. The way the echo died out in the wind, it was almost like Santa wasn't there at all. But I knew he was. Even as a small child, I knew that this moment, layered with glee and urgency, was fleeting. Nonetheless, I brushed off the heaviness of recognizing temporary bliss. Memories of these times were magic to me.

However, as I got older, I came to understand that Santa was just a myth, a fantasy meant to exhibit a beautiful and wistful façade of the holiday spirit. I never held it against my father or blamed him for wanting his daughter to live the magic of Christmas firsthand. In fact, he performed this routine with all his children. I have half brothers and sisters who are many years younger than me, and as a result, I got to see a new type of magic—the spirit of Christmas through the eyes of an adult. Like the urgency of putting the presents under the tree while Dad was out listening for Santa with the littles. Or the chaos and panic the adults felt as they arranged the "more important gifts" toward the front of the tree.

I became the facilitator of the magic.

My stepmother, who was more of a sour candy than a marshmallow, was quick to instruct family members where to place each present.

"That doesn't go there, Hon!" she'd bark at me from across the room.

"Hurry, people! Santa's almost run his course!" she'd joke with my grandma, who would sigh and take a sip of her fifth watered-down rum and Coke.

We all scrambled until just before the magic would unfold. Dad would walk in with the littles, all of them gleaming with the same magical feelings I used to feel. As they tore through their gifts, I sat back and enjoyed the beginnings of adulthood. The main thing I learned from my childhood in New Jersey with my father is that feelings of bliss can often be fleeting.

***

My ambitious and adventurous mother, motivated by the simple prospect of what any form of change could bring to her life, proposed a secret plan to me when I was thirteen years old. She threw her arms up in the air like she was on a rollercoaster and squealed, "Florida or bust, Baby!" I agreed.

This spontaneous choice to move to Florida, while exhilarating yet slightly nerve-racking, forced me to pick a parent, which is an unfair and determining decision for a child to have to make. Choosing Florida meant choosing my mother. My fragile father internalized that decision, and it complicated our relationship from that point forward. It introduced resentment and silence into our relationship.

Upon my resettlement in the Florida swamps, weeks went by without a phone call from my father. Although I was not surprised by his silence—which I simply attributed to his general flightiness and aloof nature—I was able to preoccupy myself with the novelty of a new lifestyle. Mom and I set up camp in our condo. We ate buffalo chicken sandwiches and slices of Key lime pie at local diners to properly acclimate ourselves "like real Southerners," we said. One time out at dinner, I joked with my mom, "Santa would've called his kid, you know? He's got that responsible, father-figure vibe, for sure."

My mom's eyes smiled as she sighed before speaking and stabbed the pie crust with her fork.

"He called, you know?"

I took another bite of pie. Then another. Mouth full, I managed to mutter, "When?"

"Last night. He asked me if you could stay with him for the summer. He wanted to check with me first. I said I'd ask you how you felt about it."

I aggressively picked at my finger nails, fidgeting in the booth like an anxious child.

"Is this something I need to do?" I asked her.

"Absolutely not," she grinned, and hesitated slightly, "but it might be nice for you two to reconnect. You haven't spoken in a while."

"I know we haven't, but whose fault is that?" I snapped back.

"Hey! I get it, okay?" My mom quickly dropped her fork and lifted her hands above her head. "I'm not the one who hasn't picked up a phone in months. Cut me some slack, okay? All I'm saying is, give the guy a chance. We know he's not great with expressing his feelings."

I knew she was right, but I just sat there, gritting my teeth, rolling my eyes, and scraping at the pie until there was not a minuscule crumb remaining.

***

I quit Catholic school years prior, but the symbolism of the forty days and forty nights I spent with my father and his family was not lost on me. My biblical knowledge was relatively intact, and the effects of Catholic guilt had fully taken hold.

This was my first trip to their new upstate house. My sour-candy stepmother was eight months pregnant. We were all shocked by her sudden desire to carry a child so late in life. Regardless of the fact that she and my father had adopted two children a decade prior, I was still struggling to digest this vision of her as a maternal figure. I'd watch my father fetch her an O'Doul's while she rubbed her acrylic nails against her bulging belly, swaying away in her rocking chair. I noticed she never said thank you to my father, and my father never asked that of her.

As the days slowly ticked by, the abrasiveness of my stepmother's words accelerated. She was increasingly short with my father and slightly more vocal with my half siblings. During my little sister's bath time, the shrill of my stepmother's voice echoed through the house. "Scrub behind the ears! I am so sick of you not understanding how to clean yourself! Do you *not* understand this by now?"

"Hey, Dad," I whispered to him across the kitchen table. "Is she feeling okay?"

"Yeah, she's doing well," he said as he skimmed the papers sprawled out in front of him.

"Oh, okay. She just seems a little…" I hesitated, choosing my words carefully, "…unhinged."

He managed to glance away from his papers and took a deep breath. I could see the metaphorical wheels turning in his brain. It was times like this when it was so clear that I was my father's daughter. We were both intellectuals, wordsmiths in our own right, carefully tiptoeing around the land mine that was my stepmother.

"Some people are born with an edge. You and I are not one of them. But *she* most definitely has an edge."

I accepted his analysis of my stepmother as a fair judgement, knowing that this was simply an excuse for her behavior. For the next several days, tensions ran high. The littles were coined "The Bickersons." Her word was the law of the land. My father did his best to soothe the tensions, but he was always overpowered by her aggression. This family dynamic I had stumbled into mirrored a balloon, the weighing pressure of my siblings' disagreeable nature mixed with my father's passivity was ready to burst. It was only a matter of time until my stepmom's hostility and bitterness popped that sucker wide open. Accepting my role as an observer, I plugged in to my music and took mental notes of the disarray before the storm.

Fortunately, having dodged the land mines for a full thirty-five days, we were nearing the end of summer. Only five more lunches, five more movies after dinner, five more required daily exchanges with my stepmom. This balloon was truly on the brink of bursting. But I had a plan. I told my mom over the phone that I would just sit and remain quiet, smile, say good morning and good night, and skate by until I was boarding my flight back to Florida.

For lunch that day, my dad grilled up some burgers, which we ate off paper plates. Real authentic summertime memories in the making. We sat at the kitchen table as my father rummaged through the refrigerator. Before I took a bite of my burger, I asked, "Hey, Dad, can you grab me the ketchup, please?"

Before my father even had a moment to reach for it, my stepmother's shrill voice smacked me clear in the face.

"Why don't you get up off your lazy ass and get the fucking ketchup yourself?"

Her hand was lifted above her head. Her eyes were bulging from their sockets. The littles continued to bicker at the table, clearly conditioned to overlook their mother's volume and irrationality. That's when I realized this was it. The moment. The storm. The bursting of the balloon.

Burger in hand, I locked eyes with Dad and held my breath. I waited for him to say something to her. I waited for him to put her in her place. I waited for him to defend me. But that never happened. In fact, my father remained silent for the duration of the evening. Even after I had gotten up out of my seat and walked outside to hide my tears, I never heard him speak on my behalf. I never heard him speak at all.

But he did place the ketchup on the table.

***

Nearly a decade later, after years of failing to make amends, my family and I found ourselves sitting in a run-down funeral home in South Jersey. Surrounded by cherry-stained paneling and an aroma of must, my father stood by my grandfather's side, looming above my grandmother's open casket as they both silently shared their goodbyes with the woman they both loved so deeply.

Without warning, my grandfather left the world to join his bride exactly one week later. My father found himself preparing to deliver his second eulogy in seven days. I watched him mentally rehearse his speech, clutching the tattered slip of paper in his hand. His lips did not move, but I saw the concentration on his face, his expression was a grimace laced with both focus and pain.

"Speaking at these things is not my strength, and I am sorry that you all have to listen to me for a second time in a week," my father mumbled with his head in his hands. "My father was always the one to speak at these types of things, and he always did a bang-up job, so I will try my best to do him justice." He spoke of my grandfather's many accomplishments. "But his greatest accomplishment," my father said, "was making us all smile. Christmas time was such a joy for us all, and forever onward, he will be known as the greatest Santa who ever lived."

Maintaining his composure, my father crinkled his speech into a ball, shoved it in his pocket, and sat down next to his brother. I was sitting several rows behind him, consumed with my own confusion. My stepmom took a seat beside me. While I cried unapologetically, she reached over to hold my hand, an attempt to console me, which I allowed.

***

"Open up another bottle!" my stepmom shouted at my father, as she delegated the distribution of wine at the South Jersey Country Buffet. "Hon, we're gonna need more red. Find some more red!"

Through tears and laughter, and several glasses of wine, we all relived the beauty that was Grandma and Pa's marriage. My father swirled the wine in his glass, gracefully and hypnotically. Then he asked me, "What's your favorite memory of Pa?"

"Santa, of course. By far, the best childhood memories of all time," I said without hesitation. My dad chuckled while fixating on the swirling wine.

"Yeah, he was just such a curious man," he said. "He almost had this magical quality about him."

I looked at him, continuously swirling that damn wine in his glass, and I no longer saw a silenced man. I no longer imagined him running from a monster. What I saw was a scared child, missing his father just like I had been missing mine.

WRONG NUMBER
L.A. Jefferson

It's not every day a girl learns that her father has changed his phone number and has no intention of giving it to her. Like she's some girlfriend that he's had a falling out with. Or worse, like she's the pestering ex-girlfriend who keeps calling him from different numbers so he can't block her.

Not only was I furious but I was also inconvenienced. My dad and I had been coasting along in what I perceived to be a fairly decent relationship. During the years he didn't have a car, I let him drop me off at work and use my SUV to get where he couldn't reasonably ride his blinged-out Schwinn bike, mainly fishing trips. In return, he'd keep my son on days when there was no school or an early dismissal. We were there for each other like any normal parent and child.

It was June. The school year was a few weeks away from its end. Like many public schools, my son's was spending their remaining funds on field trips. Dad had agreed to either chaperone or pick him up. I couldn't remember which one. I called the night before to remind him. No answer. I wasn't alarmed—Dad never forgot these things. If he had answered, he would have said as much.

The next morning when I called, worry set in. Again, not because I thought he forgot but because I realized that my call wasn't actually going through. I could have easily assumed the phone was disconnected, as Dad hadn't been the most responsible bill payer, but there was no robotic-like voice on the other end saying, "We're sorry. The number you've called is unavailable…" There was nothing.

My son and I finished getting ready and headed for the car. We decided to stop by the house Dad was renting, which was on the way to school and my work. Always a little behind schedule, there wasn't a whole lot of time for this visit. School began at seven thirty, and I had to be at work by eight. But I decided to drive by for my own peace of mind.

I pulled up along the curb in front of the house. A proud owner of his own SUV now, Dad was standing by the rear bumper, preparing to engage in one of his favorite summer pastimes—something outdoors, either bike riding or fishing.

"Hey, Daddy! I've been calling you. Is your phone off?" Time was of the essence.

Dad's expression was indifferent. "No, my phone is not off. I changed my number."

"Oh, okay," I said, not surprised. Dad had been getting some annoying calls from an ex and unwanted text messages from a longtime female friend. I guess he'd finally gotten tired of it. "Well, why didn't you call to give it to me?"

"I'm not giving it to you," he said frankly.

Huh? I wanted to believe that I had heard him wrong, but as an uncontrollable, angry shiver began traveling from the pit of my stomach up through my fingertips, I knew I hadn't.

"What do you mean you're not giving me your number? Why? How do you expect me to keep in touch with you?" I rambled off these questions without pause because I didn't want to hear his responses. What could he say to explain such lunacy? Not giving your daughter your phone number? Who does that?

A father who feels unloved and cast aside.

Your mother got you all in the divorce, he liked to remind us. The "all" included my older brother and younger sister. Dad and my sister had a big blowup months earlier in which she kicked him out of her house because he'd shorted her on their agreed-upon weekly payment. The anger she expressed that day had built up from all the times he'd let her down. Most notably, missed school graduations, and more recently, her wedding. Dad never considered the hurt he dished out on others.

On the other hand, my brother had never fallen out with him. My brother had worked only ten of the forty years he'd been on this earth. He was currently the DVD man in the hood, lived with our mother, drove her car, and had fathered two children. He'd grown tired of always being criticized by our father, who was no angel himself.

Of course, we all wanted my brother to work a legitimate job, but it was his choice. Unlike my father, the rest of us were able to look past his faults and recognize that, if nothing else, my brother loved and showed love to his children in ways he always wanted from our father, and he was a genuine good guy. Dad was only able to see what wasn't right with him. My brother wasn't mad at my dad like my sister was; he just chose to keep his distance.

I was Dad's favorite. At least, I would have been if he had one. My mother called me "Larrykins," an endearing variation of my dad's name. I was definitely most similar to him. We had the same problematic skin, long pointed nose, bushy eyebrows when unkempt, and obsession with health and fitness. I was my dad, without the unforgiving spirit and perpetually dissatisfied disposition.

I was the one who did not choose sides in my parents' divorce. When he moved back into our family home after a fifteen-year separation under the guise of reconciling with my mother, I was the only one who didn't believe that he had an ulterior motive. Even after the foreclosure notices started coming and he and my mom were no longer on speaking terms. Even after she filed for divorce and I'd heard through the family grapevine that he'd said, "I wasn't about to let her have that house that I've been paying for." I still didn't believe he would do that to us. Instead, I put on rose-colored glasses, telling myself that he was putting on a mask of bravado to save face in front of family.

He wasn't about to admit to anyone that he hadn't planned to let the mortgage get so far behind. All of my life, he'd played the dangerous game of letting the mortgage get a few months or more behind. Then he'd hit a lick with the lottery or work some overtime. And blam! He'd catch it up. The bright-eyed, little girl in me didn't want to think that her dad could be so devious and manipulative.

Months after our family home was gone, I made a conscious decision not to abandon him again. It's not something I like to admit, but the fifteen years that he and my mother were separated, I had essentially abandoned him, spending ninety-nine percent of my available time with my mother, not him.

Although my dad lived in the same house as me for the first seventeen years of my life, not seeing or talking to him on a regular basis was not unusual. Aside from our family weekend outings to the movies, occasional music concerts, and plays, Dad was always working his job at the automobile factory. He'd work his regular eight to ten hours followed by all the overtime he could get. And since he usually worked the afternoon or midnight shift, he was rarely at home the same time we were. As a staunch disciplinarian, his mantra was "I am not your friend," so when he was at home, my siblings and I made a point to stay out of his way. Unknowingly, we'd carried that mindset into our adult lives.

Mom was a different story. Just as when we were kids, Mom was always there. She was intricately involved in our lives. She helped out with our children during the week and on weekends. Because she worked with the school system and was off during the summer, her house was where the kids were dropped off and picked up from June through September. It was also the place where we spent holidays; Christmas, Thanksgiving, and Easter were all at Mom's.

My husband was the one who was able to change my outlook. As a noncustodial father, he opened my eyes to a man's side of a divorce story. Even if a man was at fault for the dissolution of his marriage, he can hurt just as much as his wife and children. He's already losing his partner, someone with whom he'd planned to spend the rest of his life, but when he loses his children too, he can feel blindsided and devastated.

I was ashamed that I had subconsciously chosen a relationship with my mother while convincing myself that my father didn't have the same need and desire for a relationship with me. The day he refused to give me his phone number was the same day that I, after drying up the stinging tears, decided to make that up to him.

I started randomly driving by his house on the days I knew he was off work. At sixty-four years old, Dad didn't believe in sitting around. He was always doing something, so there was no guarantee he'd be home. I tried anyway.

Given his love for the outdoors, it made catching him at home on a warm and sunny day particularly challenging. Regardless, I stopped by on the days that were convenient for my schedule. When he was home, we enjoyed a nice visit. On the days he wasn't, I'd leave a note in his mailbox: Hey, Dad, I was here.

I took a lot of flak from my sister in particular.

"You still playing Daddy's games?" my sister would ridicule on the rare occasion our father came up in conversation. There was no comeback. Despite my determination to show my dad love, I did sometimes feel ridiculous dropping by his house unannounced because I couldn't call ahead like most normal people do. But I forged ahead.

Just when I was getting used to this routine, Dad surprised me with a phone call. An *unblocked* call.

"You proved your love to me, my Love," he said, addressing me with the sweet term of endearment that melted my heart.

All was right with the world when he called me that.

"You can call me whenever you need or want to." His pride gushed through the phone as if he was awarding the Presidential Medal of Freedom.

Thank God, I thought. Our weekly visits were nice, but my life was busy. I was a wife, mother of a busy Boy Scout, and active in my church and sorority. There was always something going on. I didn't have a lot of free time for leisure visits.

With his number programmed in my phone, I quickly pulled back on my visits to his house but opened the door of my own home. Dad would come over to watch the TV programs I recorded for him throughout the week. He had a basic cable package at his house that didn't include the numerous programs that he *had* to keep up with.

My husband and dad got along great, which was a bonus to this newfound father-daughter relationship. We were like one big, happy family. Most times I didn't even mind catering to a second man in my home. I made sure to have Pepsi, his favorite beverage with dinner, and some milk to accompany dessert. We alternated with me cooking or him bringing dinner with him.

For a little over two years, Dad became an extended part of our family. My husband, son, and I met up with him to celebrate Veteran's

Day at his favorite neighborhood burger joint. On his birthday or Father's Day, we'd meet him at one of his favorite steak restaurants. But it wasn't until Dad gave me a physical birthday present—he hadn't done that in twenty years—that I began feeling like the "daddy's little girl" I always wanted to be.

Unfortunately, the feeling didn't last long. Dad went on a weeklong trip with his siblings to visit his aunt for her ninetieth birthday. If he hadn't been estranged from my brother and sister, it would have been a nice trip for the four of us. We didn't talk the whole week he was gone, so I figured that's why his answers were short when I called upon his return to see how the trip went.

"It was good," he said, not relaying any of the exciting details I'd seen posted on Facebook.

I called him another time after that, maybe a week later, and received no answer.

Oh boy. Here we go again, I thought sullenly.

I called the next day. No answer again, and no call back.

Finally, he called a few days later. "Hey. What's going on, Dad? I've been calling you," I said, hoping frustration didn't linger in my voice.

Whatever was going on with him, he never admitted. Instead, he pretended that he didn't realize he'd missed my calls. That only increased my anger and frustration.

Who had time to play these emotional games with their father of all people? I was a married woman with married-woman issues. On top of that, my husband was battling a recently diagnosed chronic illness. Dad must have been suffering from something; what it was I didn't know. He'd never been diagnosed, but my aunt, his younger sister, linked his strange behavior with exposure to Agent Orange while in the military. Whatever his issue was, I decided that I wasn't responsible for fixing it, nor could I let it have rule over my life.

Today, Dad continues to keep his distance from me. His number is still the same, but he doesn't answer my calls. Progress? I don't know. Not a day goes by though that I don't think of him. How can I not? He's my dad. Whether it's in his heart or not, it'll always be in mine. I'll always be Daddy's little girl.

UNSUNG JA-MERICAN BATTLE
Brooklyn Brand

Childhood

Daddy was imprisoned when I was four years old. Sad and confused, I remember talking to him on a phone through a glass window at a county jail in Florida. The next time I saw him was in an Alabama prison, and after that, Pittsburgh. My life with him as I knew it was over. Upon his release, he would be sent back to Jamaica, where he was from. He would not be allowed to return to America.

The last memory I have of him in prison was when I visited him with my uncle and cousin when I was twelve. I remember walking into the prison with a snaggletoothed grin and a ponytail high up on my head. Mom had me dressed nice, as usual. Daddy stood in his tan jumpsuit eagerly waiting to see us. After a long, genuine embrace, he told us the ways he was trying to get out of jail sooner.

Eventually, we wouldn't visit as much. It was too far from our Florida home. Phone calls would replace visits and become the main way we communicated. "You have a call from Dilon Brand from Florchester Correctional Institution" became commonplace for me to hear on the other end of the receiver in my young years.

In addition to the calls, Daddy sent me two cards a year, one for Christmas and one for my birthday, which were four days apart. Sometimes there was a special typed or handwritten note inside. He'd underline words like "loving" and "special" twice for emphasis. The cards were always addressed to Miss Brand, which made me feel important. My parents were always big on giving cards to express their love. I never grew tired of reading the kind words he sent me. One of the last cards read:

Because God so loved the world, he blessed me with a lovely and beautiful daughter like you.

Love you always and forever,

Daddy

Despite whatever was going on in my life, whenever I got those cards I felt special. I kept all of them tucked away in a purple book bag so I wouldn't lose them. Although I loved getting his cards, they also reminded me of his absence.

Adolescence

As I grew older, I observed in wonderment the father-daughter relationships of my friends. I'd see them laugh together at TV shows and chat about sports. I started thinking about what it would be like to have my dad around the house when friends were over or to have him pick me up from school. When I was a cheerleader, a friend of mine on the squad was routinely hugged and kissed by her dad. All I had were cards. I began to want more.

Those feelings were magnified on special occasions, especially when I watched my mom struggle financially. It was hard for her just to pay the rent, much less afford the extra things I wanted to do. When I made the cheerleading squad but couldn't raise enough money for my uniform, my mom's best friend chipped in.

Whenever he could, Daddy would ask a friend or my uncle if they were able to send us money. But my uncle made promises he couldn't keep. He promised to buy me a car. He promised to buy school clothes. Sometimes he'd only honor his word after weeks of chasing him. I remember one time he brought me money the day before school started, and Mom and I had to shop at the last minute. She was stressed, and I cried. That's when the resentment began, not toward my uncle, but for my daddy.

Even though the calls and cards continued, my birthdays felt especially empty. Christmas of 2003 was rough. Mom didn't have a dime to her name. We were living with her friend at the time. I was turning sixteen. While I was grateful we had a place to live, I just couldn't understand. I cried until my eyes were swollen and asked God why. Why couldn't I have a family like everyone else? Why couldn't I have a dad whom I could depend on to help and comfort me?

I felt fatherless. Our relationship was a far cry from normal. I couldn't simply pick up the phone and ask for advice. So many things that a daughter needs from her father were just not an option for me.

Despite this turmoil, I made it through high school and was accepted to college. But it turned out that college was just another reminder of how tough life was for me without my daddy. I didn't want to burden my mom. It was already difficult enough for her as a single parent. It was hard to tell who had it worse. I know now it was terrible for both of us; we just experienced it in different ways.

Our financial struggles continued. I tried to get my first car on my own, but I had to take it back twice due to financing. Where was my dad? He was supposed to help guide me in these situations. Through these trials the truth became ever clearer to me. He couldn't help. This bitter realization pushed me to become independent and figure out life on my own. However, as my independence increased so did my resentment.

Early Adulthood

In 2010, I graduated from college. It was not only a momentous day for me but for my whole family. We'd dreamt of this achievement for years. Yet amidst all the happiness, there was still a void. Here was another milestone Daddy was missing.

My oldest brother understood my sadness and decided it was time for me to see him. He had recently been released from prison and deported back to Jamaica.

I agreed to go.

***

My passport lay on the bed ready for a new stamp. I was eager to check this trip off my bucket list and create some new positive memories. My royal blue suitcase sat on the floor of my old bedroom at my mom's house. I stuffed it with summer clothes, anxious about what I would wear for our reunion. Green, yellow, and black outfits dominated my wardrobe as I wanted to be sure to embody a Caribbean flare.

The two-and-a-half-hour plane ride seemed more like ten hours. Admiring the fluffy white clouds against a perfect blue sky out the window wasn't enough to calm me. Neither was my brother's presence. I sat straight up in my seat with my eyes closed. I didn't know what to expect once the plane landed. It had been ten years since we'd seen each other. I was no longer the skinny twelve-year-old he'd last seen in the Pittsburgh prison. Now I was a five foot one, twenty-two-year-old woman. Would this meeting with Daddy be awkward? Emotional? I didn't know what to expect.

Once through the gate at Customs, Daddy gave me the tightest bear hug I've ever had. "Me longed to see you!" he said over and over in his Jamaican way. He teared up, and in that moment, there was no resentment, anger, disappointment, frustration, or sadness. I was as happy as he was! I just kept thinking how good it felt to be reunited. Sadly, it didn't take long at all before eighteen years of abandonment crept in. I tried to remind myself to stay focused on reconnecting and being free to enjoy the trip.

Besides spending time with Daddy, one of the main things I was looking forward to on the trip was the food. The first stop was Juici Patties restaurant where I got my fill of authentic Jamaican beef patties, coco bread, and carrot juice. Later in the trip, the sister of one of Daddy's friends cooked up some homemade oxtails, rice and peas, and cabbage. I sucked the bone clean on each oxtail! These were positive experiences not only with my daddy but with family who hadn't seen me since I was born. We also visited the well-known Jamaican tourist spot, Dunn's River Falls where my brother and I rode Jet Skis and splashed through the turquoise waters.

But, oddly enough, one of my most treasured memories happened one night when I was stepping into the shower. I pulled back the shower curtain and screamed, "There's a frog! Daddy, there's a frog in here!" I hadn't called for his help since I was four years old. He raced to the bathroom to fetch it out for me. Even though I was a grown woman, in a towel, standing next to a man I barely knew, I felt comforted and more secure because he rescued me from that frog. I finally got a glimpse of what it felt like to be dad and daughter together.

Adulthood

Six years after that reunion, the distance between us had returned. Our relationship was failing. In place of sending cards, Daddy started asking for money. The height of my frustration was when he asked me to help pay for an engagement ring for his girlfriend. It took me a month to respond because I was so fed up and angry.

I was done stuffing my feelings and not telling him how his behavior hurt me. I finally decided to tell him how hurt I was from his lack of interaction and appearing to care only for his own survival. I made it clear I wanted a better relationship and that we could work hard to make it unbreakable. He was nearly in tears, but for me, the airing of my feelings was liberating. I realized that was what I needed to do to find my peace. I just had to open my mouth and tell him how I felt and let the relationship develop from there. Of course it was rocky and awkward after that talk, but not long after, more calls started to pour in from Daddy. We even mixed in some video chats.

I stopped treating our conversations like a chore. I took the initiative to fill him in on the little details of my life like I do with my mom. He started asking me to send him copies of my work and pictures of my life so he could be more a part of what's going on with me. I was giving him more of a chance to be a father to me.

Usually, I am the type of person who holds stuff in when a situation is painful, but this was too important to me. It was something I felt needed to be fixed and could be fixed. Life is too short. I began to see some of my friends lose their dads before they had a chance to reconcile, and I didn't want that to happen to me. I believed we could make it work, so I decided to give it a chance.

Our last visit was in October of 2017. I once again made the trip to Jamaica and once again he greeted me with his customary long, tight hug. Both of our eyes filled with tears, but this time there was no resentment. I think every woman who has a troubled relationship with their father should consider reaching down inside like I did and looking for what's really bothering them and then make a decision about whether to have that difficult conversation.

While there are still many miles between me and my dad, there is much less distance between our hearts. It has become a whole lot easier for me to call him Daddy.

THE UPRISING
Lennon Carlyle

I stared at our Christmas tree's twinkling stars. The artificial snow was enchanting. We lived in the South, so the fake flakes were the closest thing I would have to a white Christmas. I was nine years old, and I remember how tiny and safe I felt lying on the soft shag carpet as the fireplace crackled. Daddy was stretched out on the sofa in his long johns as we watched *Sanford and Son*. The TV flashed a glow against the den's brick walls.

I heard a faint groan and then sniffling.

"Daddy, are you all right?"

He cleared his throat. "Baby Doll, Daddy has been having sex with a woman at work. Sometimes I got her behind the dumpster, in the van, or out front behind the column in front of the office. Her name is Beth, and I can't wait for you to meet her. You'll like her. You know that Rod Stewart song 'Da Ya Think I'm Sexy?' That's what we listen to when we're screwing. You like Rod Stewart, don't ya?"

My nine-year-old head swam. Is screwing SEX? Why would Daddy tell me something like this? My cousin, Teddy, had told me about "the talk," but he was a few years older than me. Is this the talk? What does Mommy think about this? Is this normal?

"Daddy's going to be leaving soon because your mom caught me with Beth and wants a divorce. I'll be living with Grandma and Pop for a while until I can get my own place. You and your brother will be just

81

fine. Your mom will probably turn into a slut after I leave, but you'll be OK. Daddy's a little sad and upset, so that's why I'm feeling a little choked up."

I had begged for a flocked Christmas tree since I was a toddler. Daddy had brought this one home with pride just a few days prior. Is this why he surprised us with it this year? Was it because he had planned to leave us? That morning, it was the most beautiful thing I had ever seen. Now it was just ugly and disgusting. Tears stung my eyes. Why did I want this evil tree anyway? The tree brought my family bad luck. Now it looked out of place, shameful, and rancid. Why would Santa—or God—let this happen to us?

My mind raced for days as I reflected on what I might have done to contribute to this destruction. Is it because I led my pet pony, Pistol, inside the house one time when it was raining and cold? Maybe it's because I cried when I couldn't have a Coca-Cola instead of sweet tea for dinner last week. Is it because I sobbed when Daddy lit fireworks in the trash can after putting Bootsy in it? My sweet kitty lived through that horrible night and drew blood the next morning when Daddy went outside to put trash in the can. I laughed as the bloody scratch marks trailed down his chest—Bootsy showed him! He spanked me for laughing. I was so angry at him for hurting a defenseless cat and then hurting me for laughing at his pain.

Maybe it was Mommy's fault. Daddy got angry with her so much that he would punch the wall over and over again. I remember one time in particular. She had curled my long white-blond hair that morning and told me to wear my light pink dress, lacy socks, and patent leather shoes. She had dressed my little brother in a tiny mint-green leisure suit. Then we headed to Olan Mills Portrait Studios. My brother's angelic face beamed at the camera. The energetic photographer made us laugh with toys and silly voices. It was to be a surprise present for Daddy. That night, Mommy flashed her magnificent smile and handed Daddy the pictures. He threw them back at her, and she grew small in front of us.

His deep voice boomed, "You spent my hard-earned money on this shit? Get your skinny ass in that car, take the kids with you, and get my money back. Now! Why do we need pictures of them? We see them every fucking day!"

Mommy stayed calm. "But can't you see I'm in my gown with curlers in my hair? I can't go now. They're probably closed." Then she started crying. Her hands shook. Her big blue eyes blinked with fear.

"I don't give a goddamn. Go get my money back now."

Mommy helped us squeeze our coats on over our pajamas, rushed us to the door, and we took off for Olan Mills. The lights were still on in the studio, but the door was locked. Mommy shivered and begged the man inside to let us in. "I'm so embarrassed to have to return these, but we cannot afford them," she said.

The Plymouth Fury enveloped us in safety. We didn't know what to expect when we got back home. Mommy turned the radio to Christmas songs. "Jingle bells, jingle bells," boomed on the radio, and we sang along. She detoured through the upper-class neighborhoods where the red and green lights lulled us to sleep.

The next morning, I awoke in my Holly Hobbie canopy bed. Mommy and Daddy must have carried us inside and tucked us in. Daddy acted as if nothing had happened the night before.

"That's how daddies are," Mommy said. "They forget about their rages."

***

Eventually, he left. My brother and I cried. Although our father was mean to our mother, we loved him. He was our dad, and we knew he could be sweet—sometimes.

A few weeks passed. It was time to visit Daddy at his new apartment. He was going to pick us up. My brother and I missed him so much. Well, we missed the sweet half, not the angry half. We played around as we packed our weekend clothes and decided what stuffed animals to bring. We were afraid to go. We had never left Mommy alone before. What would she do without us? What if she got lonely or scared? Our mixed emotions left us torn about who needed us more.

Our packed bags sat by the door, the stuffed animals lying on top. We waited for Daddy. Soon it was six o'clock. He still hadn't come. Mommy turned on *Diff'rent Strokes* while we waited patiently. Eight o'clock chimed on the hallway clock, and we knew something wasn't right.

"Go ahead and put your pajamas on. Daddy must've had to work," Mommy said. We couldn't understand why he hadn't shown up or at least called.

Two weeks later, we tried it again. He showed up on time at six o'clock sharp. We had never been so happy to see headlights in the driveway. We both ran outside to hug him, our little suitcases dangling beside us. He was wearing a big gray cowboy hat. *Dallas* was the new hit TV show, and Daddy thought he could pull off the J. R. Ewing look.

He took his hat off and got down on one knee to explain, "Kids, I've got big plans tonight. You can't come with Daddy this time." He placed a dull quarter into each of our palms and kissed our foreheads. We watched him hop back in the driver's seat and pull away. I thought for sure we were worth a lot more than a quarter.

Mommy read the disappointment on our faces. She immediately grabbed us both and hugged us tighter than she ever had. "I know what we can do," she announced. "Let's go out for ice cream and then go to the airport."

That's exactly what we did that evening. We sat on the hood of the car, licked our ice cream, and watched the planes fly over our heads. Mommy always made things brighter and happier.

***

Daddy's disappointments became an expected part of my life. And as I turned into a young woman, dating men was disappointing too. To say I've had relationship issues is an understatement. Every time a man divulged his feelings for me, I shut him down. Brent was a good example. He and I dated a few months and had a lot of fun together. To me, it was pleasant and temporary, nothing serious—until a dreaded conversation came up.

"You do know I'm falling in love with you, right? I've never met anyone like you before, Lennon. I think we should move in together."

I tried to comprehend the words that spilled out of his mouth.

All I could come up with was, "Thanks, Brent! I have to go. I'm late for something."

I grabbed my keys and handbag, ran to my car, slid into the driver's seat, shut the door, and let out a deep sigh. Breathe; don't forget to breathe, Lennon. Just call him later when he's at work and leave a voicemail, like you've done with the others.

Late that night as I lay in bed, I made that call. "Brent, while I appreciate your feelings for me, I have to tell you, this isn't going to work. I don't feel the same way, and I'm asking for you not to call or contact me again. Take care of yourself. Bye."

Brent didn't follow my instructions. He was unrelenting. He sent flowers, called, and showed up unexpectedly at my job pleading for me to give it another try. I tried a different, more extreme tactic.

"Brent, I'm pregnant with someone else's baby."

"So, marry me! I'll raise the baby as if it's my own. I love you so much."

"Enough is enough, Brent. I don't have feelings for you. If you continue to contact me, then I'll pursue a restraining order."

He heard me loud and clear that time.

After repeated scenarios like this, my friends and family suggested I see a psychologist. They all thought I had commitment issues.

I poured my heart out in one appointment. The therapist said I had a common fear of abandonment. I'd built up an internal barricade, and my heart was on complete lockdown. Daddy was at the center of my problem. I shut men down before they had the chance to abandon me. I couldn't allow them to get close. They would hurt me, so why not hurt them first? I'd learned that all men were selfish and would damage me.

The therapist was right. This was how I ended all my relationships with men. I was infuriated that the root of my relationship issues were because of him, Daddy. The therapist pulled feelings out of me in that one session that I had concealed for decade. I was healed, but life with Daddy never changed much. He made appearances here and there, and he called now and again. Eventually, I stopped calling or putting forth effort to maintain our relationship.

***

Then a few years ago I got a call at work from my stepmom. "Lennon, your dad is in the hospital. They think he's had a stroke. He's all right, but they're running tests and keeping him overnight."

I felt a massive lump in my throat. I could barely swallow. I mumbled something to her on the phone and sank into my leather swivel chair. Was this it? Was I about to lose my dad? No way, I thought. He's too strong and stubborn to die. He's too mean and egotistical to be helpless and in a hospital.

My mind and heart knew what was necessary. I drove two hours toward the city where I was raised. Memories flooded my mind—some of him standing us up and others of him saying I looked just like my "slutty mom." But other memories I held that day were sweet, like the time my prom date didn't show. I had worked extra hours to afford my short shiny emerald-green dress. My hair was styled and makeup done. Daddy happened to call Mommy that night, and she told him what happened. He rushed over with chocolate ice cream and my favorite candy, and we watched *Sixteen Candles* together.

He hugged me and added reassuringly, "One day, you'll meet a guy who will never let you down." That night, he was the perfect daddy.

My heart raced as I walked down the hospital hallway. Room 122 was only a few steps away when I silently prayed and pleaded, "Please God, let him live. Give us another chance. I'll work at it, and I'll try really hard this time."

I pushed the door gently and entered the room. There he was, all alone, with the faint beeping of the monitor in the background. He lay in a thin hospital gown, staring at the TV. He hadn't heard me come in.

"Daddy?"

When I got closer, he began to cry. He reached his arms up, and I leaned in for a hug. His voice was a whispering slur, "Hey, Baby Doll. You know how much I love you, right?"

In that split second, my heart swelled up, and tears rolled down my cheeks. Something told me this was going to change our lives forever. I stayed for hours by his side. We laughed and cried over so many memories.

He was released and sent home a few days later.

***

Daddy

Today, Daddy is a completely different man. That stroke must've kick-started his heart. He's a much softer, caring, loving, and humble person. I haven't reminded him of his blatant disregard for others, mental blows, and sideswipes he so freely handed out in the past. God gave him a second chance, so why shouldn't I?

I never received Daddy's love, acceptance, approval, or time when I thought I needed it. But sometimes, God has other plans. I suppose God jolted my heart the same day Daddy had his stroke. The difference is that mine helped me to forgive and remember more than just the painful things Daddy and I went through.

When I think about it, I've learned a lot from my dad and our relationship. He was the first person to teach me heartbreak. It sounds bitter, but it's the truth. Having my childhood heart broken repeatedly helped prepare me for life's peaks and valleys. Because he chose to be absent so much in my life, he taught me to be independent. He also instilled in me a solid work ethic; he taught me that I had to work for everything. He showed me patriotism for America, this beautiful land of the free. He served in the army, and that's something for which I'm proud of my dad. He introduced me to Fred Parris and The Five Satins, The Platters, The Big Bopper, and The Rolling Stones. His taste in music was exceptional, and I'm glad he passed it on to me.

Most of all, I learned not to settle for someone like him. If I hadn't gone through this relationship with my father, then I wouldn't have realized the type of man I needed or wanted in my life. Because of his example, I married a secure, understanding, self-assured, patient man.

For that, I say thank you, Daddy, for being who you were.

DADDY'S GIRL
Roxanne

I was always a daddy's girl. From day one. My father was a handsome, strong leader, a successful businessman, and a Marine. I thought he was the greatest man ever born. I lived to please him as a little girl and a young woman. He loved me too, and what made him most proud was that he thought I was attractive and athletic, just as he had been.

I've read that children get eighty percent of their identity from their fathers. At first I thought that was a strange concept, but now I can see it. I came across this information when I was researching why my relationship with my father caused me so much pain. I loved my dad, yet his behavior and treatment of me and my family members confused me. Why was he often harsh? Why did he yell and lose his temper with those he loved the most? I needed to figure it out, so I began a journey of healing the pain my father caused in my life.

Dad was a great provider. He worked hard at multiple jobs doing his best to take care of his family. He was very loyal to my beautiful and kind mother. He was home every night, and we always had dinner together. One of my favorite memories was when he carried me up the stairs to my third-grade classroom because I had cut my toe and was on crutches. I felt so safe in his strong arms.

What confused me was the way he would lose his temper unexpectedly. Things would be going great and he would just start yelling at whoever he thought deserved his disdain. It could be Mom, any of us kids, or even strangers. He drank a lot in the evenings, but he had a rule that he would not drink before six o'clock. I think the alcohol caused his moods to be unpredictable. One minute he thought life was grand and the next someone was being cussed out for something of minimal concern. He never hit any of us that I know of, but when he was mad, we all knew it and kept our distance.

One evening when I was sixteen years old, a friend came over for dinner. Dad began cussing Mom out for making such a horrible meal. I felt terrible for my quiet, sweet mom, and I was embarrassed of Dad's behavior. Verbal abuse was Dad's response to his frustrations in life. It caused the rest of us to be careful—always watchful about what we said and did. That night at dinner, I made a personal vow that I would not marry a man who treated me that way.

I was excited to go off to college and not have to deal with Dad's bouts of anger. There seemed to be less angry outbursts when my parents came to visit me because we were focused on how much we missed each other. I attended the college my dad chose. I wanted to go to another school, but he said he wouldn't pay. I chose my college major because Dad told me I would make money in that field—his field. I earned a spot on the cheerleading squad, of which he was so proud. When I chose a roommate he didn't like, he said he would not pay my rent, so I chose a different roommate because Dad always knew best. He even picked out two potential husbands for me, but I was not attracted to either of them. Dad was a bit controlling.

After college graduation, I moved back home to save money as I had just started a new job. The yelling returned, the controlling continued. Consequently, I moved out with barely any money in the bank. I was on my own and liked it. I chose friends and relationships with people who did not show signs of anger. Unfortunately, I picked up Dad's habits of drinking too much and cussing. Not the best character traits for a young woman.

I met the man of my dreams when I was twenty-two years old. His name was Mark. We were married within ten months. Dad never liked him. Mark flew small airplanes for a living and aspired to be a pilot with a commercial airline. He didn't put up with abuse from anyone, not even his future father-in-law; thus, there was conflict. When my father walked me down the aisle on my wedding day, he whispered, "All pilots cheat on their wives."

After getting married, I had a strained relationship with my father. He was very vocal about his dislike of Mark and his family. But Mark was very good to me and never yelled, cussed, or treated me poorly. Mark's family was wonderful to me also, so I did not understand why my father disliked them so much. There was no rational reason for it. It's possible he was jealous that his daddy's girl had found another man and family to love on and enjoy. The gap between Dad and me grew. I became angry at him for the way he mistreated me, my husband, and others.

I had my first child in 1989. Shortly after, I became a devoted Christian. My faith in God grew as I studied the Bible and became involved in the church. This is something my family of origin had not embraced, though both of my parents came from Christian families. At some point, I recognized that I was having trouble with my understanding of God as a father. My experience was that fathers belittled and yelled at their children. But the heavenly Father I learned about in the Bible was loving and kind.

I had read from several authors that our impression of our earthly father often transferred to the image of our heavenly Father. Even as a child, I saw God as a mean taskmaster. Despite that, even though my dad was still difficult to deal with, drank too much, disliked my husband, and often hurt other people with his words, I endeavored on a journey to forgive him. For several years, I sought the Lord through prayer, Scripture, books, Christian friends, forgiveness, and information on fatherhood.

On one occasion, I felt led to sit with my dad and ask questions about his childhood as I wrote it all down in a journal to document his life. Dad answered all my questions, and when he told me the truth about how he was raised I began to understand why he had such anger. He had always said, "I wasn't raised up, I was jerked up." He lost a brother at age eight in a car accident, and his own father died when Dad was twelve. Those were two traumatic losses for a young boy. Dad was brought up in poverty, treated terribly by his older brothers, and ignored by his mother. As I began to have compassion for Dad and his upbringing, it helped me to understand why he was the way he was.

At a church service I attended, we were asked by the pastor to contemplate someone we needed to forgive. My thoughts went immediately to Dad. I had studied the scriptures on forgiveness, and I knew it was required of a Christian. That day, I went up to the altar where there was a cross covered in nails. Having written my dad's name on a small piece of paper, I put it on one of the nails on the cross. Many others had done the same. The symbolism of this cross in front of me in light of Jesus' death on a cross, bringing forgiveness to the world while we were still sinners, was very impactful to me.

I knew that forgiveness has great power for the one choosing to forgive. I also knew from reading Matthew 6:15 that if I refused to forgive my father, God would not forgive my own sins. The Bible asks us in Colossians 3:12–13 and Ephesians 4:32 to bear with and forgive one another and to be kind and forgiving like our Father God is with us. We must choose to forgive as the Lord has forgiven each of us. Forgiveness is releasing the person who hurt you from the debt you feel they owe you. It is not easy, but it can bring much peace to life.

Many years passed after I chose to forgive my dad, and the inner wounds inflicted by his words had been healed deep within me. I accepted Dad for who he was, though he continued to be difficult. The next thing I decided to address was the divide between him and my husband.

I had been praying about how to further improve my relationship with Dad, and I felt God was leading me to this moment. I humbly approached him, bringing a gift with me, and asked him to see Mark from my perspective. I told him how wonderful Mark was as a husband and dad over the years. Dad seethed with anger and told me, "I hate him!" I began to sob. I asked Dad to begin praying for Mark since the Bible tells us in Matthew 5:44 to love and pray for our enemies. To my surprise, he agreed. A week later he described how he had walked up to his church's altar during communion and prayed. This was a breakthrough! The relationship between my father and husband did improve from there.

Then tragedy struck. My mother passed away suddenly at the age of sixty-nine. Dad's health had not been good for years, and everyone was surprised that he had not gone first. They had been married for just under fifty years. Those years after mom died were difficult since she was the glue of our family.

Dad continued to have health problems, and my siblings and I shared the responsibility for his care. There were many doctor visits, hospital stays, and other problems to be resolved without Mom around. He became depressed, extremely lonely, and began to show signs of dementia, so we hired caregivers to help us. We all made a bigger effort to be with Dad. I skipped church with my own family and drove forty-five minutes away to attend Dad's with him. I spent the night with him every Thursday, took him to lunch once a week, and took him to see his doctor. These are some of my fondest memories of him. On one occasion at church, we sang "Amazing Grace" together while holding hands. We both had tears streaming down our cheeks.

Toward the end, Dad had caregivers twenty-four hours a day. The last time he entered the hospital, he was there for three weeks. He had contracted MRSA, and his body was filled with bacteria. The doctors tried many antibiotics. He had to be tied down to the bed because he was so confused and fought the nurses to get out of the hospital. It was heartbreaking to watch.

Even though I still had a daughter in high school and Mark traveled for work, I made the effort to see Dad every day. When the doctor revealed that they thought this was the end for him, I was enrolled in a class that taught how to help those who were dying. God's timing was perfect as I would go from class straight to the hospital and apply what I had learned. I was taught to share with the person everything you wanted to say to them. I spent the next few days telling Dad how much I loved him and appreciated all he had done for me. I thanked him for many things he had given me over the years. I sang, read Scripture, and recalled silly stories as he lay in the bed, seemingly unaware. I had learned in my class that even if the dying person seems not to hear that their spirit could apprehend and to keep talking to them as if they did understand. We told Dad he would be seeing his beloved wife soon and some of his old friends that had passed on before him. At one point I asked, "Dad, can you hear me?" He seemed unconscious, but he shook his head up and down for a yes. So we continued to speak words of love and encouragement to him as he was coming closer to the end.

The very last night he was on earth, I dressed in a long white skirt and top and brought some music with me to his hospital room. I had been a dancer all my life, and it was something my father enjoyed watching me do over the years. I played the song "Agnus Dei" by Michael W. Smith and danced my final dance for my father. I smiled and felt joyful and then began to bawl. I thanked him for paying for my dance lessons and attending all my dance recitals and again sang to him and told him how much I loved him. I told him he was free to go. We all had said our goodbyes. That last night he struggled to breathe on the ventilator. The hospice nurse gave him a clean shave as she felt sure the time was drawing near.

The next morning, I got a very early call from Dad's caregiver. She told me to get to the hospital as quickly as possible. I threw on clothes and drove there, but he was already gone. I had missed his passing by five minutes. I knew right away that I was not meant to be there when he passed on. It would have been too much. I am so thankful the caregiver, who was my dear friend, was with him in his last moments. In my spirit, I knew Dad was with the Lord and that he and my mom were reunited. Not only that but it was comforting to know he no longer suffered with the struggles of this world. He had gone to a place spoken of in Revelation 21:4 where there is no more sorrow, tears, or pain.

Raising my own children while helping care for my elderly father was tremendously wearisome, but I wouldn't have done anything different. I truly believe that because I had forgiven my father I could spend those last years with him when he needed me. My faith had allowed me to forgive. Dad never apologized for the hurt he caused in my life, but it wasn't necessary because I chose forgiveness and love that I learned from my heavenly Father. I had always been a daddy's girl, and I still was to the end. Because of my Christian faith, I have the knowledge that I will one day be reunited with Dad again in heaven.

THE TRANSITION
K E Garland

2012

"I just thought you oughta know," MJ's Arkansas drawl dragged the remaining words, "your dad has stage-four throat cancer."

What did she want me to do? My heart seethed with twenty-three years of anger. When Mommy died, he left me to fend for myself. Daddy moved on by dating a light-skinned Creole stranger. He introduced her at Mommy's funeral. He and Creole woman spent several nights together just weeks after the burial. His absence grew frequent. Sometimes he announced his intentions of "going to get laid." Other times he simply left. Three months later, for the first time in my life, I awoke to Christmas in an empty home. He introduced me to loneliness. He demonstrated the ease with which one could shift priorities.

Daddy's role in my life faded with each passing revolution, especially after he sent me to live with my maternal grandparents. Eventually, he and Creole woman married. Then, they divorced. Daddy wasn't single long. MJ replaced Creole woman and vowed to love him forever. Two decades yielded sparse interactions, unless I initiated them. It had become a game of imbalanced burden. My side often weighed heavily with calls and visits. His piece included thin, father-like appearances during major milestones.

MJ's news interrupted a year's worth of silence. It broke my conscious decision to drive to Chicago without seeing him. It disrupted my choice to sever communication: no calls, no emails, no Facebook. Before she phoned, there was little reason. Always being the so-called bigger person had gotten old, and I'd refused to carry the weight of our dysfunction.

MJ's message hung there, somewhere in between two and half decades of waning devotion and her perception of my obligation.

Weeks later, it turned to judgment. "You could send a card or something."

"Are you sure you don't want to do something?" my husband, Dwight, echoed.

Memories of where I ranked on Daddy's to-do list had hardened me. Financial support replaced care and concern for him. Dwight and I loaded a pre-paid Visa card each month to help with medication. And we found a final expense insurance plan to supplement his policy.

It was irrational for him to want more from me than he'd sown.

***

2013

So, he began to give more of himself. Though chemo and radiation captured his voice and health for six months, the following year brought frequent and authentic communication. He whispered through conversations, many times asking me to recount tales of my daughters and what they were into. The doctors felt hopeful that reconstructive surgery would repair his vocal chords and also help avoid a tracheostomy. Daddy's confident nature kept family encouraged. His optimism led us to believe that the future would hold sounds of his renewed speech.

Emotions stirred. Toward the end of that year, my family and I made our biannual trek to the Windy City. Years of tradition dictated that we stay at my great-aunt's house on the west side, spend Christmas day with my mom's side of the family, and then travel south to visit Daddy around eight o'clock at night.

"It's like you just do a drive-by," MJ once commented. "I mean you come by, but then you don't never stay long."

She was right. Her home didn't hold my childhood. Her name graced the deed years before we met. Daddy moved there after their nuptials. Each wooden step that creaked under my feet held her nostalgia, not mine. Not ours. Sure, he was my dad, but he made memories under her blue roof, not I. Most years, I did well just to stop by at all. But this holiday, a line of concern began to outline the periphery of my heart. It mattered not where he lived but rather that he survived cancer and post-ops. We created a new ritual. Dwight, the girls, and I arrived at his house during the daylight hours.

A smile spread across his face as he opened the door. He hugged each of us through our winter wear bundles. A white patch protected his throat's incision. Later, I would learn about the careful process of cleaning this wound. Blue-and-white cans of meal-replacement shakes sat on the kitchen table, some empty, others waiting their turn. Before I could sit down, he cupped my face in his palms as if I were six.

"You and I need to have a talk," he whispered.

I rolled my eyes. "Alrighty."

He winked at my family, who sat single file on the white, leather couch. "Just a little daddy-daughter talk," he reassured them.

He handed the girls the remote. I followed him up the rickety, narrow staircase to their attic's makeshift office. The black swivel chair swooshed air as I plopped down. He sat across from me on a black folding chair and leaned over. Our eyes met, his already watery.

"I feel as if you've been mad ever since your mom died."

I maintained my stoic gaze. "I used to be. But not anymore."

"What did you want me to do?"

He wanted to know what he could have done when his anger led him to pack up all of my teenaged belongings one night and throw them in black trash bags in the middle of my bedroom. He wanted to know what he could have done after he sent me to live approximately one hundred miles east in a rural Michigan township. And he wanted to know what he could have done after giving up his parental rights when I had just turned seventeen.

"You could have called to see how I was doing."

His eyes could no longer hold the tears. He removed his glasses and wept. "That's all?"

"Yep. That's it. You left me there and didn't look back."

Tears crawled down his face. "*Who* put your stuff in black trash bags?"

Chemo brain. The effects of treatment left him with selective memories. While I could never forget how my clothes and stuffed animals rested haphazardly in those garbage bags, now he couldn't recollect who'd filled them. He attempted to recall why his former self would've engaged in such an egregious act. Eventually, he determined that he must have been "really mad."

Our talk continued. I described the difficulty I'd faced defending him against my grandparents. They paid for my wedding, while I bargained for Daddy to walk me down the aisle. They funded my baccalaureate degree, while he and MJ attended, beaming with pride, as if they'd contributed. Grannie supported me through my PhD, while he primped for commencement. I did my best to explain the loneliness of losing one parent to death and another to abandonment. But it's a challenge describing experiences to a clueless perpetrator. In fact, I'd shared these stories many times before. But this was the first time he listened.

"Why did you decide to ask me now?"

He cleaned one lens, then the other. He placed his glasses back on his face. "It's the threat of mortality, Baby. Death makes you see things differently."

Our talk lasted forty-five minutes. By the end of it, my face had softened. Care crept closer inside my heart. Daddy promised to spend the rest of his life repairing our relationship. He and I set up his Skype account for frequent visual chats.

***

2014

He kept his word. Daddy assumed more of the onus of our bond. Consequently, the scales balanced toward parallel understanding. But a new barrier surfaced. Having diabetes hindered his previous throat operation from properly healing. He had to have tracheostomy surgery after all. He would be able to eat solid food. However, he'd have to learn to use a tool to talk. We Skyped. We could see each other, but his words garbled. We called. We could hear each other, but unclear phrases lingered. Life is interesting that way. The voice required to fix missing decades disappeared.

I suggested texting. He agreed. He often forgot to power his phone, and sometimes he would take several days to return a message. But overall it worked. Conversations centered on the girls, Dwight, my endeavors, his health, and when we would reload the prepaid card.

He reminded me of his promise. I'm going to spend the rest of my life making sure you know that I love you. Though I'd carved out a space for hope, a large percentage of skepticism remained. I was a forty-one-year-old, married woman. My oldest daughter was a year shy of when I'd lost my own mother. My youngest daughter had little knowledge of who "Grandpa Tony" was and secretly called MJ by her first name, instead of Grandma. Wasn't it too late for the type of mending that he wanted simply because of the threat of mortality?

Regardless of doubt, we persevered.

***

2015

Hard work and commitment heals most wounds while wrapped in the movement of time. And our recovery was no different. The daddy-daughter scale equaled compassion and concern on both sides. But past insecurities remained. I struggled to embrace a repentant father. I had one foot in therapeutic overhaul and one cautious foot out. But this experience left me little choice but to leap forward.

Soon it was May. I outlined our broken history via blog. Descriptions devoted to Daddy's role in my teenage life and lack of participation in my adult life characterized him as a deadbeat.

He was hurt.

I reminded him of our deficient relationship and assured him that these were *past* feelings, not current ones. He thanked me for the clarification. But I didn't hear from him for three weeks.

My birthday came and went. No text from Daddy. I wallowed in old emotions, and I thanked God for the noncommittal foot because no communication signaled past behaviors that I'd once endured. I reached in my bag of coping mechanisms and chose the most familiar one, detachment.

Just when I decided to disengage, my cousin's message flashed. *Mom wants to talk to you.*

Alrighty, I wrote back.

Aunt Dora revealed that Daddy and MJ had moved to Atlanta. I had no idea. She continued with pleasantries and wished me well on my family's upcoming Japan trip.

Another message glowed from my cousin. *Did you ever hear from Mom, Uncle Tony, or Aunt MJ?*

I talked to Aunt Dora but not Daddy. Little black dots rose and fell as he typed.

Do you want me to tell you, or do you want to wait? They have something they need to say, but they don't want you to worry.

I braced myself and answered, *Tell me.*

He has cancer on his lungs now, and it's hard for him to breathe.

Thoughts about Daddy melded into one glob and froze. That night, I slid under the covers and slipped into an unsettled sleep. The next morning I awoke around five, lay in bed, hopped out, and then brushed my teeth. Dwight stared from the corner of his eye, worried about my early rise.

Thoughts thawed over the next few hours and spilled into a pool of panic. What if he dies while we're overseas? They can't bury him without me. Oh no! He's gonna die, for real. This means the opportunity for a father-daughter relationship has ended. My mind shifted to childlike desires. Why couldn't I have had parents devoted to raising and being with me? Where were my quirky mom and dad who embraced relationships, grandchildren, and family vacations? Compassion cracked my heart open. Daddy had endured cancer without his only daughter. There was time and space for me to choose a different path.

Silently, I stood in the middle of my kitchen. Both hands wiped my face clean of tears. I said a prayer that his spirit and soul be at ease through transition. Then, I consciously put both feet into the relationship renovation. At this point, I wanted Daddy to know that I cared. My will to forgive became greater than decades of resentment. It was time to move on. He was right. The threat of mortality does shift one's perspective.

I texted. *Hey Daddy. Hadn't heard from you in a while. Hope you're okay.*

No response.

I texted MJ.

No response.

A few minutes later, he answered.

He described the move to Atlanta. He explained his breathing trouble. But he didn't mention lung cancer. I told him we'd visit before leaving the States. Three smiley-face emojis accompanied his *Yay*.

He was just as happy to see us in person two weeks later. But I was dismayed. A brown bag of bones stood before me.

"Never thought you'd see me this skinny, huh?" he joked, revealing several missing teeth.

His receding mini-afro had turned a snowy shade of white. He shuffled around showing me his room, bathroom, and patio. Having mastered the talking tool, his words, broken and robotic, were now comprehensible.

MJ's weariness made itself a visible part of the room's energy. Her voice trailed behind as she described the new cancer developments on Daddy's lungs. They had just found out right before they'd packed up a new life seven hundred miles away from years of familiarity. She needed directions to Emory. I wanted to ask why they hadn't mentioned the move. But somehow, it seemed meaningless.

Dwight, the girls, and I moved a few boxes to and from the outside storage. People walked directly past their porch. Third-floor dwellers peered down, invading their space.

Daddy frowned. "We need some iron bars out here."

I laughed. But sadness filled my heart. I promised to try a little harder. They were only five hours away. I had no idea how long Daddy would live. And it didn't matter anymore. They were close enough for me to offer more help.

He cupped my face in the palms of his hands.

"Come back," he whispered to me.

"I will," I promised.

But my newfound commitment was too late.

When we arrived back in the States, Daddy had an oxygen tank. He couldn't speak without coughing, spitting, or gasping for air. Shortly after, doctors refused him chemo. Frailty wouldn't allow it.

He refused to eat.

Three more days, the hospital moved him to hospice.

The next day, he was unresponsive.

My daughters and I returned to Atlanta. The nurses' soft, overly kind voices coupled with sunset lighting cued me for the end. The girls and I entered his room. HGTV blared. Deterioration set in and left a shell of his former self, absent of spirit. He lay amongst white blankets and pillows: limp, mouth open, and body angled up enough to appear as if he was actively breathing. But he wasn't. His connection to a sugar IV gave us time to make funeral arrangements. Although MJ had warned me about his coma-like state, I still tried.

"Daddy," I said above a murmur.

His breath belabored. In. Out. Gasp.

I handed the girls my car keys. There was little reason for them to witness the moment. I held his skeletal hand and regretted that I didn't accept his apology sooner. I'd wished we both could've done better. But acceptance set in. This is what was supposed to be.

The following morning, MJ and I met with the funeral home and then returned to hospice.

All the patients' doors were open, except his.

We entered. The sun's light shone through cracked blinds. Quiet filled the remaining space. No apparatus. No wires. No machine. My gaze shifted toward the window. All of his blankets were neatly folded and all of the white fluffy pillows stacked one on top of another. His mouth was still open. His body laid flat, the woven white covers neatly folded across his chest.

Daddy transitioned about fifteen minutes prior.

He seemed to be at peace. And so was I.

© 2017 *The Transition* was originally published with The Coil.

FATHER

A. E. Kitson

I know so little about you. I do regret that and I wonder if it is possible to go back while there is still time? But is there still time? And if there is, what would I ask you and would you answer me truthfully, or would you continue to evade my curious, questioning heart, confuse, abuse, lose me in that maze, that maze that you constructed, stiff, stifling, solid walls around you, saying "keep out"?

Who mothered you? Who fathered you? Who were your friends? Who struck you? Where did your rage come from? At whose hands did you learn to fight, bite, keep tight, never lose sight of the anger, hold it, nurture it, feed it, plead with it to keep you safe, safe from the hurt and the pain which surely must have followed you doggedly in your formative years?

My tears, my fears, the passing years, heaped in a pile in a bundle in the centre of my heart. I keep meaning to have a clear out, but I don't have the strength to tackle that bundle, so I trundle along in the hope that one day soon, I'll march in, take hold, unfold all those offending garments, toss them into a place where I can see them for what they are: questions, questions with no answers. No answers.

I have known you for years untold and yet I do not know you. You have been in my heart, never too far apart, lingering languidly upon my lips, in my thoughts, in my prayers and layer after layer of you is impressed upon my being. I need to forgive myself for not getting to know you. I need to forgive you for not letting me get to know you.

***

My poem *Father*, whilst not answering the questions I wanted from my father, helped me to process once and for all the need to have a relationship with the man I called my father. It made me realize that I was never going to have the father/daughter relationship I still longed for years after I had ceased to have any sort of contact with him. It gave me the opportunity to articulate my thoughts in a way that let me understand that I *could* ask the questions to which I would never get the answers. It helped me to accept that not all of us as daughters are privileged to have what we see as our right to have the 'perfect' father. The poem also helped me to let go of that longing for a father that I never had and could never have. It made me see him in the light of forgiveness because that is the only way that I could move on and move forward and heal.

CONTRIBUTORS

BB is a writer, mentor, and customer-focused pro, tirelessly devoted to serving others through words, influence, and good deeds. She's a woman who takes pride in her roles as wife, mother, daughter, and sister. She dreams of living in a world of endless pancakes where women realize their self-worth.

Brooklyn Brand was born and raised in Jacksonville, Florida, by her single mother. She graduated cum laude from the University of Florida. As a journalist, she has written stories for the web and on-air. She is happy to share her personal story outlining life without her dad's presence.

Lennon Carlyle is a freelance writer, raised in Georgia, where she currently manages an industrial equipment business. She loves meeting new people and hearing their life stories. Lennon and her husband just celebrated their ten-year anniversary. You can follow Lennon's blog at fabulouswithglitches.wordpress.com or contact her at lennoncarlyle@gmail.com.

K E Garland is an award-winning indie author whose work includes *The Unhappy Wife*. She lives in Jacksonville, Florida, where she is wife to Dwight Garland Jr and mother to Kesi and Desi. More of her writing is at kwoted.wordpress.com, and her editing services can be procured at writingendeavors.org.

Ishna Hagan creates marketing-driven website copy and e-commerce stores for North American businesses. She is also a published author—most notably for her article "Gulf Residents Protest, Brace Themselves for Effects of Oil Spill" (National Newspaper Association, 2010) and for her WUSA9 online news reports. Ishna has one beautiful daughter and is a proud Howard University graduate.

LaCharmine (L.A.) Jefferson is the author of two contemporary women's fiction novels, *Unfinished Business* (2009) and *Reconciliation to Hell* (2017). Her writing can also be found on her blog, *Naturally L.A.* (naturallyla.wordpress.com). She is a wife and mother of two. Visit her website, lajefferson.com, for more information.

A.E. Kitson was born in Jamaica and was brought up in London, England. She has worked in local government and as a civil servant. In her leisure time, she writes poetry. Her poems have been published in anthologies and newsletters: "Damaged People" (Whispers On the Breeze: When Pain Came to Stay, 2009), "When Pain Came to Stay" (In Our Own Words, 2009), and "Five Strike Fourteen" (Nottingham Women's Centre, 2009).

Charise Kollar is an English teacher by trade with a passion for mentoring and igniting a sense of self-awareness in teens. She is the co-founder of the spiritual blog for millennials, *Real Talk Universe* (realtalkuniverse.com). While she was born in New Jersey, Charise is a self-identified Floridian who has been residing in Tallahassee since 2008.

Varina Price was born in Fresno, California. She holds a degree in public health from National University and is currently completing nursing school. She is married to Nicholas Price and is mother to Aaron Peraza, Bryce Peraza, Noah Peraza, and Brayden Price.

Roxanne is a devoted wife and mother, sustaining a home of peace and respite for all who enter. She recently completed her MA in marriage and family counseling from Liberty University and enjoys helping people work through the pain of their past by means of a Christian world view.

Anna Scott believes in the power of writing our stories to facilitate healing and personal growth. She lives in New England with her husband, two children, and the family cat. "The Thing About My Father" is her first published personal essay.

Tikeetha Thomas is a full-time working mom with a beautiful nine-year-old son who is the apple of her eye. She resides in Maryland and spends time volunteering, blogging, and maintaining a healthy relationship with a wonderful man. You can read more about her life at her blog, *A Thomas Point of* View (athomaspointofview.com).

S.R. Toliver is pursuing a PhD in language and literacy education at the University of Georgia. Her current research is based in the critical tradition, analyzing young adult literature and literacy pedagogies in an effort to promote social justice and equity in education. She can be reached on Twitter: @SR_Toliver.

Kotrish Wright is a recent MSW graduate from Florida State University. She was born and raised in Jacksonville, Florida. She's also an avid traveler and believes faith, support, and resilience can get you through any storm. Follow her journey at kotrishwright.wordpress.com

www.ingramcontent.com/pod-product-compliance
Lightning Source LLC
Chambersburg PA
CBHW031559040426
42452CB00006B/359